THE
LEVENSALERS
OF
WALDOBORO, MAINE

WALTER L. LEVENSALER

HERITAGE BOOKS
2008

HERITAGE BOOKS

AN IMPRINT OF HERITAGE BOOKS, INC.

Books, CDs, and more—Worldwide

For our listing of thousands of titles see our website
at
www.HeritageBooks.com

Published 2008 by
HERITAGE BOOKS, INC.
Publishing Division
100 Railroad Ave. #104
Westminster, Maryland 21157

International Standard Book Numbers
Paperbound: 978-0-7884-1606-4
Clothbound: 978-0-7884-7081-3

TABLE OF CONTENTS

INTRODUCTION

As far back as I can remember there has been a great
deal of confusion in my immediate family on how the
Levensalers happened to come to America. They
presented a number of vague and conflicting ideas, none
of which were substantiated in any way. No one it
seems, had taken the time to document the history of a
family that had been in this country for over 200 years.
When I began to research the name and town where the
Levensalers settled, I was surprised to find that so much
had been written about the old German settlers in
Waldoboro. I sought out sources in the libraries of the
Maine Historical Society and the New England Historical
Genealogical Society with great enthusiasm and they
formed the basis for my early research. I quickly realized
that the sources I uncovered had one thing in common;
they each related the sorry tale of how the early settlers
established The Broad Bay Settlement. I find it amazing
that this hearty stock won out over such adversity. I
have included the bibliography from the Maine Historical
Society that details this early history (see appendix IV).
Of particular interest are the accounts of the settlement
in the *Pennsylvania German*.

To establish and maintain a settlement that later grew
into a major center for shipbuilding and commerce in
such an unlikely location is a source of great
wonderment. Credit must be given to the craftsmanship
and endurance of the early German immigrants and the
generation that immediately followed them. To make so
much from so little is not a common occurrence. They
developed themselves into a pool of skilled labor that was
harnessed by early English entrepreneurs to
manufacture one of the few things that was available to
them: ships! The town endured and prospered this way
for over one hundred years until other shipbuilding
areas,

such as Bath and Portsmouth, eclipsed their efforts. This is a heritage to be proud of and one worthy of the many accounts that have been written.

As my research continued, I found that the early Levensalers had very large families and began to move to areas away from Waldoboro. They traveled to towns close by: Thomaston, Camden and Lincolnville and as far away as the Mount Katahdin area. The following family history was compiled after years of searching through town records, census data, land transactions and historical accounts of the Towns of Waldoboro and Thomaston, Maine. These sources were rich with data. However, a number of unanswered questions still remain, as some of the information gathered was incomplete and at times contradictory. There are still many gaps in the data, but I have gathered enough factual information to put together a credible family story.

In the following pages you will find a general exploration of the "LEVENSALER" family, with a more specific treatment of my branch of the family. It is followed by a sketchy account of other members of the original migrating group. Then, at the end, I mention some unanswered questions. I have used the appendix section to provide background material and representations of documents that are mentioned in the text.

This history should be viewed as an attempt to memorialize the contribution the family has made to the establishment of the towns of Waldoboro, Thomaston, Lincolnville, Searsmont, Sebec, Atkinson and Abbot, Maine.

ACKNOWLEDGMENTS

During the first few years of my research, I had worked with data provided by the Maine Historical Society as well as information found in the U.S. Census records going back to 1790. The result of this study was enlightening, but left many questions unanswered. I could not connect one generation with another and needed new sources. At this point, I decided to place and inquiry in the *"Yankee"* magazine genealogical section. The response resulted in a major breakthrough in my research. I received information for the first time, of the existence of two old "Levensaler" family Bibles. The individuals who supplied me with this valuable information were Murial Mitchell of Washington, Maine, and Martha Thompkins of Waldoboro, Maine. I owe both these women a debt of gratitude. With the information they provided, and a copy of the flyleaf from the original family Bible graciously supplied by Atwood Levensaler of Concord, New Hampshire, I was able to piece together the complete succession of my family from 1730 to the present time through eight generations. The prospect of this accomplishment seemed very remote at the time.

Later, I received important information on the Christopher Levensaler side of the family from Ms. Isabel Morse Moresh of Morrill, Maine. This information helped clear up some of the mystery surrounding that part of the family. Still later, I received additional information from "Will" Whitaker of Murray, Utah, who is working on a major project that includes gathering information on the old German families of Waldoboro. He is working with the records in the Family History Library in Salt Lake City. In addition he recently sent an associate, Gary Horlach, back to Germany to study old church records. From these sources, they have provided information on the family that dates back to the seventeenth century.

CHAPTER I

THE MIGRATION

The earliest confirmed record of the Levensaler name dates back to the mid 17th century. There is a small village in southwest Germany in the province of Hessen-Nassua called Bettendorf, Rüppertshofen. Here Johannes Liebenzeller was born about 1654. Church records show that he married a woman from the same area named Anna Margaretha, who was born around 1656. Further records show Johannes died on September 1, 1728 at the age of 74, and is buried in the village of Obertiefenbach. After his death his wife, Anna Margaretha went to Alten Diez to live with her son Pieter. She died there and was buried from St. Peter's Church in Diez, the date is unknown. We know that Johannes and Anna had a least two sons:

Their oldest son, Johannes was born about 1700. He married Anna Margaretha von Friedenwalt of Obertiefenbach on June 27, 1724. There is no other mention of this couple in the church records of the time.

His second son, Pieter, was born about 1706, in the same town. He was the first Levensaler to come to America. Pieter was married to Anna Apollina Baüer on November 22, 1729 in Alten Dietz, Hessen, Germany. He is listed in the records at that time as a tailor.

Attracted by the *"Waldo Circular,"* he petitioned the government to leave Germany around 1752. In preparation, he attempted to sell the property he owned in Alten Dietz and the nearby village of Heistenbach. After a failure to sell the property at market value, the Mayor, a man named Eberhardt gave him 326 Florin, 17Alb for the titles. The record shows that Pieter's debts at the time were 129 Florin, 8 Alb. After paying his debts and his departure tithe, he was left with only 187 Florin, 9 Alb to take on his journey to the New World. We know

these facts from information gathered by Gary Horlacher
in his survey of church records in this region of Germany
in 1992. He was doing this work in conjunction with
"Will" Whitaker who initiated a history project that
started in 1991. They are researching the backgrounds
of German families that established the Town of
Waldoboro, Maine. *Although it seems certain that the
family migrated from this region of Germany, the name
itself probably comes from a small village West of
Stüttgart called Liebenzell. Liebenzeller then would be
"man from Liebenzell"*.

If you look on the map you will find that the Hessen-
Nassaü province is in South West Germany, a region that
has been disputed for centuries. Wars between France
and Germany and between various German barons often
took place here. In this environment of constant turmoil
it was extremely difficult to establish a lasting enterprise
of any kind. There was always a threat of new regime
coming to power and destroying all semblance of order.
Under these circumstances, it is easy to understand how
Pieter Liebenzeller came to be enticed by the *"Waldo
Circular" (see appendix I)*. He may have had second
thoughts if he knew what lie ahead of him. As we shall
see the early history of the Levensaler family in this
country is a story of triumph over hardship, deception
and fraud. The first settlers of the family were among a
large group of exploited and mislead Germans who
arrived in the New World with high hopes and desires to
start a new life. These hopes were soon be dashed by a
series of broken promises.

In the middle of the eighteenth century, England was in
the process of settling the wilderness territories along the
northern coast of New England. The population, at that
time, was scattered up and down the seacoast from Nova
Scotia to Portsmouth, New Hampshire, in small
settlements protected by forts. However, England's claim
to this land was disputed by the French, who with their

Indian allies, wreaked havoc on any settlement the English tried to establish.

In an effort to strengthen their claim, the English began a campaign to increase the number of settlers loyal to the Crown. This was to be done in part by recruiting Protestants from Non-English speaking countries in Europe. In keeping with this effort, General Samuel Waldo, a descendant of one of the original proprietors of the territory and subsequent owner of a sizable portion of the region (Waldo Patient) began efforts to settle his territory in the Broad Bay area of Maine.

In 1748, he began recruiting German citizens from the Palatinate region in South West Germany. As an enticement Waldo offered each settler 100 acres of land on the water with provisions for six months. He also promised to provide clergy, and protection from hostile forces that surrounded the new settlement. *This area was the original tribal lands of the Wawenocks, part of the Abenaki Tribe. These Indians were nomadic and did not have established settlements in the area, never-the-less, they saw the white settlers as intruders on their hunting and fishing grounds and had been successful for several years in driving out previous colonist.*

It is difficult to understand the thinking of Waldo and Listner when they planned the German migration of 1753. They had known that previous attempts to settle the region had failed because of inadequate preparation and the immigrants of 1742, 1751 and 1752 were languishing. Yet they established a company of Southern Germans that were not familiar with pioneer life and set out to sea at the end of the growing season to land in hostile Indian territory with no garrisons and inadequate quarters to carry them through the first winter.

The most disturbing aspect of the entire venture was the way they used these people to establish their claim to the land. We can assume that most of the German

immigrants were uneducated and somewhat naive.
Because of this they would have relied heavily on the
word and counsel of their religious and political leaders.
To believe the leadership would knowingly send their
constituents into such a deplorable situation is
unthinkable. The "*Waldo Circular*" was nothing more
than a misleading advertisement that duped both the
leaders and the eventual immigrants; to think that this
country was settled by such misrepresentations and
cunning, is appalling.

In my view, the proprietors gambled very little and
received much for their investment in the establishment
of this colony. The settlers were required to pay for their
passage, were given poor living conditions aboard ship,
where eighteen died, and had to endure the first winter
in a totally inadequate quarters called a "long house",
where seventeen more died. The settlers were on their
own to make or break the venture with their very lives at
stake. They in fact, took all the real risks and the
proprietors and Crown received most of the benefits.
Where is the memorial for these poor souls? Does such a
group of gritty, courageous and determined people
deserve some recognition in the general history of the
nation or should this just be passed off as condition that
all pioneers in this country faced?

At this writing there is a mystery as to the whereabouts
of the remains of many of the first settlers. Some claim
that there may be a mass unmarked grave somewhere in
town. Others speculate that there may have been an
option given to the first settlers to return to Germany or
to be settled some where else in this country. The
disturbing thing is why does the uncertainty exist? How
can so many lives be lost without a trace? The oldest
gravestones in the Old German Meeting House Cemetery
are those of the children of the original settlers i.e. Maria
Eleanora Levensaler and Conrad Heyer, where are the
parents? This family history unfortunately does not
answer these questions, but only makes note of them.

In any event, with this promise of free land, the Pieter Liebenzeller family, signed on to come to America. They, along with other German families, which included the Benners and Shümanns, started their migration in the Spring of 1753 by traveling down the Rhine River to the embarkation port of Amsterdam, Holland. They sailed from Amsterdam on the ship *"Elizabeth"* with Captain Pendock Neale on July 16, 1753.

The Ships' Passenger List, as found in the *"Knox Papers,"* is entered as follows: *(see appendix II)*

To: Broad Bay, Maine:
Pieter Lievenzöllner, Tailor
Wife: Apollenia (Bauer)

Son: John Adam	Age	23
Dau: Catherina	Age	21
Son: Georg Willem	Age	14
Dau: Anna Maria	Age	12
Son: Christoff	Age	09
Dau: Anna Margaretha	Age	07

After stopping to pick up additional passengers in Cowes, England, they began their twelve week journey across the Atlantic, arriving on October 6, 1753 off the coast of Maine at the St. Georges' River. During the crossing; of the 258 passengers, eighteen died aboard ship and three babies where born.

What a shock it must have been to see the settlement for the first time, thinking there was some kind of established village only to find a few crude cabins. That first fall and winter, the new settlers stayed in a compound prepared by Karl Christopher Leistner, a representative of General Waldo. This compound was located near "Benner Hill" in Broad Bay. Historical accounts of that first winter tell a sad tale of death and hardship as the promised provisions and shelter, were totally inadequate. Eaton in his *"History of Warren"*

describes a "long house," where the settlers were housed
their first winter, that had no fireplace or chimney, and
could not be heated properly during the cold weather.
Many men, women and children perished that first
winter and it is claimed that they are buried in a mass
grave located somewhere near this disastrous site.
Unfortunately this grave is not marked and has not been
found at this writing. Some evidence of the general living
conditions of the settlement around this time can be
gleaned by reading the petitions the people sent to
Governor Shirley of Massachusetts in 1754 and 1757
(see appendix IV).

In the Spring of 1754, the settlers of "1753" received
their promised land in Broad Bay on the East side of the
Medomak River in the area that is now East and North
Waldoboro. Not all the land was directly on the water as
promised, but in many cases was unbroken wilderness
several miles inland. However, each settler did receive
100 acres of land and for the most part, each lot had
some access to a water supply. In this same year,
General Waldo began construction of a stockade at
Sprouls' Spring, for the settlers protection. There is an
opinion that although the settlers where allowed to settle
on this land, they were never given title. (Eaton claims in
his "History of Warren" that they were merely given a one
hundred year lease on the land with an option to buy).
The "Waldo Circular" does not mention these conditions,
although this may be closer to the truth. The settlement
became stable, grew and established itself in spite of all
the hardship; fighting off Indians while at the same time
planting and harvesting crops.

It is clear that the Liebenzeller family was not prepared
for the ordeal that lay ahead of them when they arrived
in 1753. The father and sons were tailors, craftsmen and
artisans. They were not equipped for a hostile pioneer
life in the wilderness. All the same, it seems that two of
the sons, Christoff and Johan Adam, and one daughter,
Anna Margaretha, married shortly after their arrival, and

settled on their own farm. The record shows further that Johan and Margaret (Anna Margaretha) persevered and remained in America until they died, while Christoff may have returned to Germany sometime before 1780. I believe that all the Levensalers living in this country today, with the various spellings of the name, are descendents from this original family headed by Pieter. Some will dispute this claim, but I feel the records are clear enough to support this belief.

There is no further historical record of the father Pieter, his wife Apollenia or his son, Georg Willem and his daughters, Anna Maria and Catherina in the records of the Broad Bay settlement or in the U.S. Census. However, records do place Pieter in Boston in 1759 as a sponsor at the baptism of his grandson in King's Chapel. This leads to some speculation that Pieter never settled in Broad Bay at all, but moved on to Boston with his wife and younger children to ply his trade as a tailor. They became part of the "Lost Generation" as some of the first settlers have been called.

In 1763, at the end of the last French and Indian war, when peace finally arrived at the settlement, a Mr. Shem Drowne presented himself along with a group of Pemaquid Heirs (Seth Sweetser, Thomas Drowne, Alexander Nickels and John Savage) to the citizens of Broad Bay. They had with them a *"Power to Act"* that gave them a claim to a vast area of land including the land West of the Medomac River in Broad Bay. They based their claim on the Pemaquid Grant dated in 1657. This, of course, pre-dated the Waldo Patent. Much of the claimed territory was settled by the German immigrants of 1748 and 1752 and was land promised and received from Samuel Waldo in good faith. *(The immigrants of 1753 did not seem to be involved in this claim, as most of them had settled on the East side of the Medomac.)* After the presentation of their claim, on September 21, 1763, the Pemaquid Heirs executed about fifty deeds with the settlers for land they had thought to be their own at the rate of two Schillings, eight Pence per acre. A small group of settlers, however, refused to voluntarily recognize the claims made by Drowne. Seeking a resolution, the Pemaquid Heirs pursued the issue through a Committee set up by the Massachusetts General Court. Unfortunately for the settlers, General Waldo had died in 1759 and his heirs had no interest in the land. As a result, they did not actively dispute the claims of Drowne and some even agreed that the Waldo Patent did not extend to the West Side of the river. This left the German settlers at the mercy of a government committee that favored the propertied class. As expected, in 1765, the General Court, indicated without giving a formal decision that they favored the claims made by the Pemaquid Heirs. This caused the land on the West Side of the river below the falls to be released to the Pemaquid Heirs. This decision was not received well by the dissident settlers in fact they became so incensed by the action of the General Court, they vowed never to pay for land that they believed was rightfully theirs and refused to deal with Drowne or the other Heirs.

If this wasn't enough, other proprietors, embolden by the success of the Pemaquid Heirs came forward with claims of land ownership in the Broad Bay area causing the settlers to defend their claim once again. This activity was too much for some of settlers to bear, so that in 1773, a group of farmers sold their farm equipment and livestock, burned the farm buildings and houses, strew boulders into the fields that they had previously cleared, and otherwise made their land less valuable for the disputed landlords. Many in this irate group moved to Londonderry, South Carolina to a settlement their fellow countrymen had established. The Pemaquid Heirs received an average of 10 pounds for each farm that was *"purchased"* in this way. The General Court Committee's non-decision was blatantly unfair and without merit, but typified the attitude and treatment meted out by the British gentry prior to the Revolutionary War.

This episode did not end the land troubles in Broad Bay. A new claim on the land came after the Revolutionary War. Land ownership on the other side of the Medomac River came into question. As it happened, in 1768 the Waldo heirs sold all the remaining unsettled land and lots on the East Side of the river to Thomas Flucker for a fair market price. He died before the end of the Revolutionary War but left his land holdings to his daughter, Lucy. Normally, this would have been the end of it, for all British land claims would be voided after the Revolutionary War. But Lucy had married Henry Knox, who had become an American war hero. In 1788 the couple decided to move to nearby Thomaston and General Knox began to actively manage the property left to his wife.

Over the years many settlers on the East side of the river had taken control of the unassigned lots in question and began farming and using them as if they were their own, thus assuming possession. Knox's agents began pressing the General's claim to these lands and asked the *"squatters"* for compensation or to stop their use of the land. At this time, Knox's agents counted one hundred and one settlers on land claimed by General Knox.

As time went on, some of the settlers came to an agreement with Knox's agents and made an accommodation. However, over sixty others could not come to an agreement. This stalemate situation become intolerable for the towns people and in 1803 they petitioned the Governor to set up a Commission which would operate on its own terms to settle the property rights of the deputed lands and set out a schedule of payment. Knox agreed to abide by the decisions of the Commission, while a total of sixty-one settlers submitted their claims. On October 19, 1803 the Commission published their decision, which predictably found in favor to General Knox and set out a schedule of payment for all sixty- one squatters. Among these last holdouts was Peter Levensaler and Jacob Benner, who had to pay ninety dollars with interest for their 50 acres of land listed as plan number 23.

CHAPTER II

JOHAN ADAM LEVENSALER

Johan Adam Leibenzeller was born on January 30, 1731 in Alten Dietz, Hessen-Nassaü, Germany. He has been and deserves to be called the patriarch of the Levensaler family in America. Being the eldest son of Pieter, the original immigrant, he became the executor and head of the family when his father died. The history of the settlement of Broad Bay is strange in that it mentions Johan from the start but never mentions his father Pieter even once. In fact some of the historical accounts of the town give Johan credit for the deeds and activities of his son and grandson both named John. Doing so, the historians have payed no attention to the fact that the events are more than 100 years apart. (So much for the preciseness of historical accounts).

Shortly after arriving in Broad Bay in October of 1753, Johan married a fellow passenger of the "Elizabeth", Marie Elenora Shühmann.

Maria Elenora's family is listed in German records as follows:

Father:	Johan Nicolaus Schumann (1711-1769) est. Born: Bergen/Kirn, Idar-Oberstein, Palatinate, Germany
Mother:	Anna Catherina (1713-1800)est.
Brother:	John Bernard (1730-1800)est.
	Maria Eleanora (1732) Born: Lowen nr. Breslau, Silesia
Sister:	Maria Louise (Lucy) (1734-1786) est. Later Married Friedrich Schwart, February 23, 1755, Trinity Church in Boston.

Brother: Philip Jacob (1742-

Sister: Maria Elisabeth Henriette (1745-

It is not clear whether Johan and Maria began their marriage living on the 100 acre farm promised to Pieter or on their own 100 acres. It seems that Johan would be entitled to his own farm because he was over 21 when he arrived in Broad Bay. In any event, what is described as the original family homestead, a 100-acre farm on a site that is now North of the Harold Rider farm in Waldoboro, was sold to Barnabus Freedman for $675 in the late 1750's.

The union of Johan and Maria produced a large family of nine children; first five girls then four boys. Among the boys were twins Adam and George.

After helping to establish the original farm and village stockade, Johan became a member of the "Home Guard" or Militia. In 1757 the record shows that from May 16th to October 31, 1757 he served under Captain Jonas Fitch as a yeoman. The Home Guard was set up to defend the settlements against French and Indian attack. He was paid Eight Pounds, One Schilling for his service. *(See Appendix IV)* His name is listed third from the bottom on the muster roll and is spelled Leavinfeyler. At this writing, this seems to be the extent of Johan's military service as there no record of him serving in the War of Independence. After the last Indian War, when the area became more secure, Johan moved away from the first family farm and settled on the old Elias Hall Farm in Waldoboro, a piece of land next north of the current railway station.

During the 1760's not much is written about Johan as he was busy establishing his new home, farm and family. He surfaces again in 1772, when he and his brother, Christopher were two of the signers on the deed that established a site for the new Lutheran Reform Church. The Church was to be located across the river on the East side of town away from the church headed by the discredited Pastor Schaeffer.

By the 1770's Johan had become one of the leading citizens of Waldoboro and perhaps was looked upon as an elder at the time. During this decade he took on political duties. In the first published list of town officers (September 21, 1773) he is listed as a Surveyor of Highways. Later in the 1775 listing of town officers he is listed as The Third Selectman.

In 1788 Johan purchased land from John Benner in what was to become the Town of Nobleboro.. He established a home on this land and lived there until his wives' death in 1798. Reading the first U.S. Census in 1790 we find Johan listed with his wife and four sons and one daughter. *(See Appendix III)*. Four of his daughters: (Christina, Maria, Katernia and Anna Margaretha) had already married and were living in separate households at that time.

Because of Johan's influence and his family's interest and participation in education; in 1793 when the first school districts in Waldoboro were laid out, the general North Waldoboro area was called the *"The Levensaler School District"*.

On December 19, 1798, Maria Eleanora died in Waldoboro and was buried in the Old German Meeting House Cemetery. The headstone is located just behind the church and is one of the oldest markers in the cemetery. The simple inscription on the stone reads as follows:

> *In Memory of*
>
> *Marie Elenora Levenseller*
>
> *Wife of John Adam Levenseller*
>
> *Died Dec. 19, 1798*
>
> *AE 66 Yrs.*

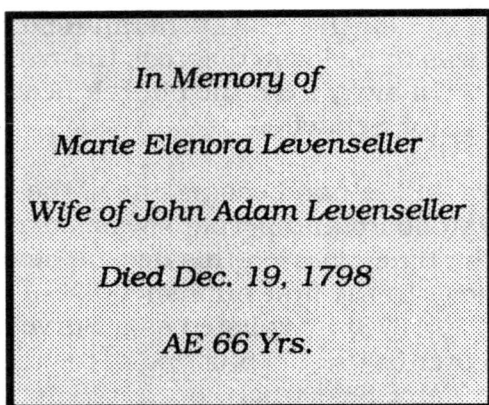

Because this is the only writing on the stone, we can surmise that she is buried by herself.

After his wife's death, Johan transferred all his remaining property to his sons, and traveled to Boston. We do not know of his activities there, until an obituary appears in the paper on September 3, 1799. Johan died in Boston on September 2, 1799. *(See Appendix IV)*. The Boston burial records for this period have been ruined by water, so that at this writing it is not possible to trace the cemetery in which Johan is buried. However, we do know that he was buried from The Trinity Church in Boston and is interred somewhere in one of the old cemeteries of the city.

Johan never saw the turn of the century nor did he live to see the final settlement of his land holdings from the various proprietors of Waldoboro. These final land settlements were completed in 1830 and were made to his sons George and John. Through Johan's and Maria's suffering and hardship a substantial family was established in the New World that has endured for over 230 years. In the early days the Levensalers were farmers, craftsmen and seamen. Their children have since become doctors, lawyers, teachers, and businessmen. Such is promise of the "American Dream".

Note: *Some claim that the name Levensaler is an Anglicized version of the German name, **Löwen zöllner;** which literally translated to English means "Tax collector from Lion". There is no way to substantiate this interpretation however.*

JOHAN ADAMS' CHILDREN

Listed in birth order as recorded in the family bible in the possession of Pauline Levensaler of Concord, New Hampshire:

Christina -
First child of Johan and Maria, was born on August 4,1755, in Waldoboro. Married Peter Leicht III about 1770. Peter was born on February 5, 1752 and was baptized on February 6, 1752 in Oschelbronn, Germany. He was in the Revolutionary War,enlisted at Waldoboro in 1777 Campaign against Burgoyne. He died in1837 in Waldoboro. They had eight children:

1. Peter Light born about 1771. He was in the War of 1812. He married Anna Newbert abt.1798.
2. John Light born 1772, died October 27, 1873. He married Anna Shuman on February 4, 1799.
3. Daughter born 1773
4. Daughter born 1775
5. Daughter born 1777
6. Andrew Light born 1785. He was in the War of 1812. On May 7, 1807 he married Abigail Leeman. He died on June 7, 1871 and is buried in Brookland Cemetery in Waldoboro.
7. Francis Light born 1788. He was in the War of 1812. He married Huldah Moore on September 15, 1808. He died sometime after 1820.
8. Adam Light born in February, 1791. He was in the War of 1812. He married Margaret Castner on August 8,

1815. He died on January 6, 1872 and is buried in the German Cemetery.

Maria -
Born, November 17, 1761 in Waldoboro, Married John Neubert on December 23, 1787. Died about 1814. John was born on July 25, 1762. He served in the Revolutionary War as a private in Col. Wheaton's 4th Lincoln County Regiment raised on August 20, 1778 for service in the campaign in Providence. He died on July 28, 1851. They had ten children:

1. John Newbert Jr. born on August 25, 1788. He was in the War of 1812. He married Sarah Miller on September 3, 1814. He died on October 31, 1860.
2. Mary Newbert born on August 25, 1788. She married Henry Storer on May 26, 1821. She died on November 26, 1833.
3. Michael Newbert born February 21, 1790. He married Susan Mank on January 11, 1821. He died in 1882.
4. Adam Newbert born December 6, 1791. He married Dorothey Storer on October 6, 1824. He served in the War of 1812 and died on March 4, 1866.
5. Elizabeth Newbert, born September 24, 1793. She married Robert Rokes in 1826. She died in 1840 in Appleton, Maine.
6. Margaret Newbert, born November 21, 1795. She married Moses Richards in 1818.
7. Jane Newbert, born January 16, 1797. She married John Rokes in 1819.
8. Peter Newbert, born October 27, 1798. He married Catherine Benner on February 14, 1829.
9. George Newbertm, born July 6, 1801. Died August 1869 in Waldoboro.
10. Anna Newbert, born July 6, 1803. She married Jotham Davis in 1823.

Katerina -
Born July 8, 1764 in Waldoboro. Married John
William Proct on November 17,1787. Died on
February 23,1850. John Proct was born in 1759
and died on December 19,1844 in Waldoboro. They
had at least four children:
1. John Proct, born in 1793. Married Nabby
   Dinsmore on January 18, 1819 in Waldoboro.
2. Elizabeth Proct, born 1794. Married Eliphalet
   Jones on April 9, 1811 in Waldoboro.
3. Anna Proct, born 1800 in Waldoboro. Died on
   September 19, 1821.
4. Peter Proct born in 1803. Married a Sarah A.
   in 1846. Died October 26, 1858 in Waldoboro.

Anna Margaretha -
Born September 30, 1766 in Waldoboro, Married
John Martin Benner on March 31, 1786. Died on
October 20, 1854. John was born on May 15, 1764
and died on May 15, 1844. He is buried in the
Comery Cemetery. They had eleven children:
1. Catherine Benner born October 3, 1786.
2. John Benner born November 21, 1788. He was
   in the War of 1812. He married Margaret Ann
   Feyler on November 4, 1813. He died on
   October 16, 1856 in Liberty.
3. George Benner, born April 18, 1790. Married
   Sarah Schwartz on February 25, 1825. He
   died on October 20, 1848.
4. Eleanor Benner born November 28, 1793.
   Married Jacob Clouse on March 31, 1814. She
   died in 1870.
5. Elizabeth Benner, born March 6, 1795.
6. Adam Benner, born September 2, 1796.
   Married Jane Kaler.
7. Peter Benner born August 27, 1800. Married
   Mary Ann Levensaler on October 27, 1827.
   Died on March 31, 1885.

8. Simeon Benner born May 12, 1803. Married
   Sarah Bornheimer in 1831. He died on May
   18, 1891. Buried in Comery Cemetery.
9. William Benner, born November 27, 1806.
   Married Mary Creamer on June 22, 1845. He
   died on July 19, 1852.
10. Zenas Benner, born March 25, 1809
11. Isaac Benner, born November 16, 1812. Died
    on October 7, 1841 in Liberty, Maine.

Elizabeth -
Born July 1, 1769 in Waldoboro, Married George
Proct on August 15, 1793. Elizabeth died on
February 25, 1849. George was born in Broad Bay
in 1765 and died on February 10, 1845. They had
seven children:
1. Catherine Prock, born 1794. She married
   Fredrick Schwartz on February 24, 1821. Died
   on April 2, 1887.
2. Elizabeth Prock, born 1801. She married
   Charles Sides on April 30, 1821.
3. Solomon M. Prock, born 1802. He married a
   Caroline in 1831.
4. Israel Prock, born in 1803. He married Sally
   Schuman on September 27, 1824. He died on
   March 11, 1881 in Waldoboro.
5. Bathsheba Prock, born 1807. She married
   William Keith in 1829.
6. Sally Prock, born 1809. She married Frank
   Frederic Benner on September 14, 1844.
7. Eleanore M. Prock, born 1811. She married
   Isaac G. Benner on October 15, 1835. She
   died on June 12, 1869.

Adam -
Born April 15, 1773 in Waldoboro. Married Mary
(Polly) Turner on May 5, 1798. Died June 16,
1849. More details follow on this large and
prosperous family.

George -

Born April 15, 1773 in Waldoboro as Adams' twin. He married around 1813 and lived his whole life on his farm in Waldoboro until his death in 1844. He is buried in the Commery Cemetery in Waldoboro with his wife Margaret (Sides), who was born in 1777 and died in 1857. Some of their children are buried with them: Loring, Amos and Sally. His daughter, Mary married Frederick Overlock in January of 1823. Early U.S. Census records do not provide the name of his other children, so his history remains incomplete.

John -

Born January 30, 1775 in Waldoboro. Married Kathern Achorn on January 8, 1799. Died on February 14, 1845. More details to follow.

Peter-

The youngest child of Johan and Maria was born on April 6, 1778 in Waldoboro. He married Elizabeth Kinsel on January 10, 1803. Elizabeth's mother (Betsy) was born in Germany on June 12, 1746, her grandfather Johannes was born there on February 22, 1709 and the grandmother, Mary Elizabeth Jung was born on September 16, 1714. In 1804, Peter was forced to buy the 50 acres of land he was farming for $90 after General Knox had his prior claim upheld. He is mentioned in 1809 town documents as a Hog Reever. Peter served in the War of 1812, when he was mobilized to defend against a possible landing of British troops in Camden Harbor. *(see appendix IV)*. Peter and Elizabeth gave their children the middle name of Kinsel thus allowing us to trace some of their descendants. Peter lived to be almost 85, he died on February 8, 1863 outliving his wife, who died on January 9, 1862. Both are buried in the Rural Cemetery in Waldoboro with their daughters Bersha and Jemima.

THE THOMASTON CLAN

ADAM LEVENSALER

Adam Levensaler, twin of George was born on April 15, 1773 in Waldoboro. At the age of 25 he married Mary (Polly) Turner of Waldoboro on May 5, 1798 (Mary Turner is reputed to be a descendent of one of the Mayflower pilgrims). *(See details that follow.)* After their marriage they moved to Thomaston, Maine where he worked as a cooper for General Knox. He purchased land and built a house near the Oyster River in that town. Adam lived his entire life in this one location and raised ten children. He died in Thomaston on June 16, 1849 at the age of 76.

Adam is survived by a large and prosperous family, who played an important part in the development of the town of Thomaston. The current spelling of the name can be attributed to Adam, who used this version as early as 1840. Adams descendants have moved far and wide, some moved to California in the mid 1800's and established a large family there, others moved South to New Orleans. It is assumed that this family traveled to these far off regions not over land but by sea. A great many of the Levensalers living today are descendants of Adam and his brother John having twenty children between them.

By most measures Adam was the most successful second generation Levensaler. He raised a large family of prominent and industrious children. Intermarriage with other leading families in town served to enhance their position even more. In reading Cyrus Eaton's *"History of Thomaston"* one can appreciate their contribution to the development of that town. The following is a brief outline of two generations of Thomaston Levensalers with some pertinent notations taken from that book. Looking at the following data one can see the affinity these Levensalers had to marry women with English ancestry, as well as their love of the sea.

MARY TURNER (1773 - ?)

Mary Turner married Adam Levensaler in Waldoboro, Maine on May 2, 1798. She is probably a descendant of a passenger on the *Mayflower*. She was born in November of 1773 in either Hanover or Bristol Massachusetts. Her family moved to Waldoboro, Maine around 1778. Her father Cornelious, was a shipbuilder in Waldoboro and served as a selectmen in 1794 and 1804. He was born on May 5, 1741 in Hanover, Massachusetts and married Mical Sylvester there on December 8, 1768. After 28 years of marriage, she died in 1796. Then, at the age of 57, he was remarried to Abigail Soule in 1798. He died in 1830. Cornelious's ancestry is as follows:

Father:

Caleb Turner II (1722-1767)
Married: Ruth Barker

Grandfather:

Caleb Turner (1697-   )
Married: Rachael Dwelley, October 27, 1713

Great Grandfather:

Thomas Turner II Resided in Sicuate, MA in 1680 Married: Hanna Jenkins, February 9, 1695

Great Great Grandfather:

Thomas Turner living in Higham as early as 1637. Married: Sarah Hilland, January 6, 1652. Thomas was probably a passenger on the *Mayflower*.

THE ADAM LEVENSALER CHILDREN

BARDEN T. LEVENSALER

Barden; Adam's first born arrived the same year that Adam and Mary were married in 1798. The record shows that he married Ann James Robinson, on August 21, 1828. Ann was born into this prominent Thomaston family on May 25, 1800.

In a listing of Militia officers, Barden is listed as a ensign on June 26, 1823, a lieutenant in the light infantry on August 28, 1823 and a captain on September 12, 1827. Barden died in Thomaston on June 4, 1852

The birth order of their family is as follows:

William B.
Born in Thomaston on June 10, 1829. He married Anastasia Hanley of Bristol on December 18, 1859 and they resided in Boston where he is listed as a mariner. Their child, Florence N. was born in April of 1860

Hester A.
Born in Thomaston on March 11, 1831. Died at the age of eleven on September 23, 1842.

Edward R.
Born in Thomaston on April 21, 1833. Worked in Thomaston as a painter. There is no record of marriage or death.

Thomas H.
Born in Thomaston on November 12, 1834. He worked at sea as a mariner. In 1861 he joined the Navy as a seaman and saw action in the Civil War. There is no record of marriage or death.

THE HONORABLE ATWOOD LEVENSALER

Judge Atwood Levensaler was born in Thomaston on November 8, 1799. He married a prominent Thomaston women, Nancy Coombs on January 28, 1831. Nancy was born on September 17, 1807. They raised a large family of nine children. Nancy died on December 8, 1862. Atwood practiced law in Thomaston and held many appointments and honorary positions, among them are: 1833 he was a Selectman and Chairman of that body for several years. Town Counselor in 1842 and 1843, and Deputy Collector of Taxes. He represented Thomaston in the State Legislature from 1836 to 1838 and from 1845 to 1855. In 1839 to 1840 he was appointed State bank Commissioner. In 1843 and 1844 he was one of the Governor's Executive Council. Was chosen one of the Trustees of Thomaston Maine Academy and was also its Secretary. In 1857, During the Presidency of James Buchannan he was Deputy Collector of Customs for the Port of Thomaston. He was also the President of the Thomaston Mutual Fire Insurance Co., holding that office until his decease. Among some the other offices he held was the Commissioner of the State Prison and member of the International Boundary Commission. He was a very prominent, active and efficient debater, an active politician, a Democrat of the Andrew Jackson School. After the death of his wife he retired and led a more quiet life. Atwood died in Thomaston in June of 1869.

The birth order of his family is as follows:

Henry C. , M.D.
Born in Thomaston on April 15, 1831. Graduated from Bowdin College as a medical doctor. He married Mary Elizabeth Starelle on October 25, 1866. He practiced medicine in St. George, Maine. He is listed as a member of the Natural History Society on March 16, 1859. During the Civil War

he was appointed Assistant Surgeon of the 19th Maine Regiment and was later promoted to Surgeon in the 8th Maine Regiment.

Mary T.

Born in Thomaston on October 15, 1832. She married Thomas S. Andrews on November 30, 1863. He was a member of the construction firm of Levensaler & Company and worked there as a joiner. Resided in Thomaston. There is no record of children or death.

John C.

Born on May 7, 1835 and worked as a cashier in the St. Georges Bank. He married on November 26, 1866. There is no record of the wife name or date of his death.

Augusta

Born in Thomaston on January 7, 1837. There is no record of marriage or death.

Adam P.

Born in Thomaston on April 13, 1839. Worked as a mariner out of Thomaston.

Atwood J. Levensaler, Jr.

Born on March 3, 1841 in Thomaston. Married Nettie Prince Cushing, who was a direct decedent of Mayflower passengers, (see detail to follow) on August 30, 1869. They had three children: James born in 1871, Eliza born in 1875 and Alfred (detail to follow) born in 1876. Atwood was a clerk in the Thomaston, Maine Bank from 1855 to 1858. Became a bookkeeper in the A.A. Creighton store for the next seven years. In 1869 he was in partnership with his father-in-law in the J.O. Cushing Company, a manufacturer of lime. He was a prominent member of the Democratic Party; elected Moderator of Town Meetings for 25

25

consecutive terms without opposition. An almost
constant delegate to the Maine Democratic
Conventions. Repeatedly offered the nomination for
candidate of the Democratic Party to represent in
the State Legislature, but always declined it.
Democratic candidate for Senator in 1876 and
1880. In 1884 President of the Democratic State
Convention, and candidate for Governor of Maine in
1886. In 1889 was appointed by Governor Burleigh
as *Commissioner of Centennial Celebration of the
Inauguration of George Washington* as president. He
delivered the Address of Welcome at the Centennial
Celebration of Thomaston in 1877. He was a
popular speaker, ready debater and always an
impartial Presiding Officer.

HENRIETTA CUSHING (1851 - 1936)

Henrietta Cushing married Atwood Levensaler in
Thomaston, Maine on August 23, 1869. She has quite a
remarkable pedigree and is worth noting. Both her
mother and father came from decedents of the
passengers on the *Mayflower* in 1620:

Henrietta's mother was Clementine Woodcock (1825 -
1894). She traces her lineage back to William and Love
Brewster both passengers on the *Mayflower.*
  Magaret Waning (-)
  Nathan Woodcock (1793 -)
    Rebecca Healey (1757 - 1813)
    Nathaniel Woodcock II (1748 -1826)
      Nathaniel Woodcock I (1707 -) *
      Mercy Bewster (1708 -)
        Nathaniel Brewster (1676 - 1755)
        Mary Dwelly (1648 - 1764)
          William Brewster (1645 - 1723)
          Lydia Partridge (- 1742)
            Love Brewster (1611 - 1650)
            Sarah Collier (1615 - 1691)
              William Brewster (1566 - 1642)
              Mary Wentworth (1568 -1627)
*Nathaniel Woodcock was reported to be a great Indian fighter and
owner of a blockhouse in Attleboro.

Henrietta's father was James Otis Cushing (1814 - 1894)
he was a shipbuilder and lime manufacturer in
Thomaston. He traces his roots back to the *Mayflower* in
the following way:

Dr. Isaiah Cushing (1777 - 1819)
Hannah Vose (1780 - 1816)
  Seth Vose (1733 -)
  Rachael Copeland (1749 -)
    David Copeland (1704 - 1750)
    Elizabeth Bent (1707 -)
      William Copeland (1656 - 1716)
      Mary Bass (1669 -)
        John Bass (1632 -)
        Ruth Alden (1634 - 1674)
          John Alden (1599 - 1687)*
          Priscilla Mullin (1602 - 1685)**

*Tradition has it that John Alden officiated over the marriage of his
daughter, Ruth to John Bass. At the time, John Alden was listed as
a wheelwright and living in Bridgewater and Duxbury.

** There are also claims that Priscilla Mullin's mother died the first
winter after the *Mayflower* landing.

Alfred W. Levensaler:

Was born on May 15, 1876 in Thomaston, Maine.
He married Mary Williams, born on August 22,
1868 in Washington, D.C. They were married on
August 18, 1909. Alfred resided in Washington,
D.C., Kensington, Maryland and finally in
Concord, New Hampshire. He graduated from
Bowdin in 1902 and Harvard Law School in 1906.
Alfred died with his wife on the same day on May
9, 1952.

    Atwood Levensaler: Who up until his death on
February 6, 1994, had original family bible in his
possession, was born on April 10, 1911 in
Washington, D.C. He served in the U.S. Army
from 1943 to 1946 in the Pacific Theater. On
August 23, 1941 he married Pauline Leavitt of
Concord, New Hampshire in Hartford,
Connecticut. Pauline was born in from Canaan,
New Hampshire on December 29, 1913.

Orris

Born in Thomaston in 1843, died a year later on
October 1, 1844.

Nancy

Born in Thomaston on June 12, 1846. Married on
September 2, 1877. There is no record of death.

Lucious

Born in Thomaston on January 8, 1850. Died at the
age of four on January 20, 1854.

LINCOLN LEVENSALER

Adam's third son was born in Thomaston on April 30,
1801. There is no record of Lincoln's occupation but it is
known that he spent his entire life in Thomaston. He
married Angelica H. Jenks, (born in 1814) in 1834. In
1829 he shot a 200 pound deer which was a record at
that time. He is listed on the committee to build a new
church (First Universalist). He was part owner of the 81
foot, 148 ton schooner *"Iowa"* built in Thomaston in
1840. Lincoln died on the original family homestead on
January 12, 1863. Not much is known of his large
family of eleven children. Many of the children did not
survive to adulthood. The birth order of their children
are as follows:

Frederic

There is no record of a birth date, marriage or death.
It is noted, however that he was a mariner.

George D.

Born in Thomaston on December 13, 1836. Worked a
clerk in Thomaston. There is no record of marriage or
death.

Julia F.

Born in Thomaston on October 28, 1838. Resided in Boston. There is no record of marriage or death.

Francis B.

Born in Thomaston in 1840. There is no record of marriage or death.

Sarah A.

Born in Thomaston on April 6, 1842; died a year later on July 26, 1843.

Charles L.

Born in Thomaston in 1843. There is no record of marriage or death.

Caleb II

There is no record of birth, marriage or death.

Lydia

There is no record of birth, marriage or death.

Thomas J.

Born in Thomaston on January 18, 1846. Died at the age of 12 on September 29, 1858.

Catherine

Born in Thomaston on October 5, 1847; died about a year later on September 21, 1848.

John West

Born in Thomaston in 1850. There is no record of marriage or death.

JULIA S. LEVENSALER

Julia S. Levensaler was born in Thomaston on October 25, 1802. She became the second wife of Thomas

Howard. Thomas was born in 1792 so that he was ten years older than Julia. They were married on July 1, 1830 and resided in Waldoboro on land that is across from his families' homestead. Howard ran a blacksmith shop opposite this land. Thomas died on October 21, 1867 at the age of 75 years, 3 months, and 3 days. Julia died thirteen years later on September 21, 1880 at the age of 77 years, 10 months, and 26 days. Their children are listed in birth order as follows:

Samuel
Moved to New Orleans where he died of yellow fever on August 7, 1858 at the age of 26 yrs. He was buried in Thomaston on March 18, 1869 after his body was exhumed in New Orleans and transported to Maine.

Julia L
Born in Thomaston in 1832 and Died July 4, 1854 at the age of 22.

Lincoln
Went South to New Orleans and then to Texas. He married and resided there. He died on November 8, 1865 at the age of 20 years, 5 months, 24 days.

William C.
Married, engaged in trade, and resided in Galveston, Texas.

Sarah F.
Resided in Waldoboro Village. Died on August 14, 1919.

Orris L.
Died November 8, 1865 by a fall from the masthead of a brig in Thomaston.

CAPTAIN CALEB LEVENSALER

This seafaring man was born in Thomaston on August 14, 1804. Caleb was to marry into the Gilchrist family, who were famous for shipbuilding in Thomaston. This marriage set the stage for their children who also married into a famous shipbuilding family, the Chapmans. Caleb married Harriet Gilchrist on June 9, 1832. Harriet was born in nearby Camden in 1808. There is no record of Caleb death but the record does show that he was involved in building a series of ships:

Year	Class	Tonnage	Name	Builders	Chief Owners
1834	Brig.	203	*"Raymond"*	F. Seiders	Gilchrist, Levensaler
1840	Sch.	149	*"Iowa"*	Mortons	Levensaler Carney, Abbott
1848	Ship	746	*"John Hancock"*	W. Stetson	Gilchrist, Snow Levensaler
1855	Ship	1035	*"J.F.Chapman"*	R. Walsh	Walsh, Chapman, Levensaler
1859	Ship	1050	*"Montebello"*		Levensaler Webb, Walsh

Captain Caleb was a master mariner and captain and thus became part owner of these ships.

His children in birth order are as follows:

Elsie

Born on September 28, 1832 in Thomaston. Married Edmund B. Chapman on June 17, 1855 and they resided in Thomaston. Edmund was born on July 27, 1827. He was a shipbuilder for the firm of Levensaler, Walsh & Co. He died on July 20, 1858.

Olive R.

Born on November 11, 1834. Married Captain James Chapman on June 30, 1858 and resided in Thomaston.

Joseph G.

Born on April 19, 1837 and worked as a mariner out of Thomaston. He married Emma Adams, who is reputed to be an ancestor of the famous photographer, Ansel Adams. Their children were: William, Caleb, James, Burgess and Lewis. Some of these boys later moved to California, perhaps during the "Gold Rush". Joseph died in 1914.

Harriet

Born in 1844. There is no record of marriage or death.

Raymond

Born in 1850. There is no record of marriage or death.

LEANORA LEVENSALER

Adam's second daughter, Leanora was born in Thomaston on September 15, 1806. She married a man who was 48 at the time, on November 10, 1833. His name was William H. P. McLellan. William's first wife, Eliza Clough died on November 16, 1854. Leonora and William resided in New Orleans. Their marriage was stalked by tragedy. All three of their children died before they reached the age of ten. William died after only nine years of marriage on October 8, 1842. Their children were:

Charles Henry
Died on December 17, 1839, 2yrs. 4mos.

Franky
Died on May 8, 1855, 8yrs. 3m. 11 days.

ELSIE K. LEVENSALER

Adams' third daughter was born in Thomaston on January 14, 1809, died on August 12, 1862 in Waldoboro at the age of 53. There is no record of marriage.

MICHAL LEVENSALER

Born in Thomaston on November 19,1810. Died on March 2,1817 at the age of six.

SARAH F. LEVENSALER

Born in Thomaston on December 17,1813. She married John S. Coburn no record of children or death.

CAPTAIN ORRIS LEVENSALER

Adam's youngest child was born in Thomaston on January 17, 1817. He died tragically at sea on February 11, 1843 at the age of 26 when the brig *"Raymond"* went aground on Absecon Beach, New Jersey.

THE WALDOBORO CLAN

JOHN LEVENSALER

John was born on January 30, 1775 in Waldoboro. Some historians claim that his middle name was Godfrey thus confusing him with one of Chistophs' sons. I have not come across any records showing him to use this name. He married Kathrine Achorn on January 8, 1799 and began to raise a large family of ten children. With the help of this large family he was able to operate an extensive farm in North Waldoboro near Benner Corner. A notation in the town tax record of 1822 characterized the farm as being so large that it took three yoke of oxen to work it. John served as a town selectman for four years (1835-1838). He prospered as the town grew and was able to assure his children a good start in life. Records of old business transactions show the John sold goods to many people in the village including some very prominent citizens. Among them being Mr. Isaac Reed, who designed the Maine state seal.

John received an inheritance of land from his father, Johan Adam, and purchased additional adjoining farmland. He added still more through marriage, in this way he developed one of the largest farms in Waldoboro. This farm was located in North Waldoboro on what is now State Highway 220, North of U.S. Route 1. Running through this land is "*Levensaler Brook*" just south of Benner Corner. This "*Belscap*" area had enough population to warrant its' own school district. It was named the "*Levensaler School District*" in the seventeen-nineties. John successfully worked this farm with his ten children for over fifty years.

There seems to be an implied agreement between John and his sons which in substance meant that the boys would work the farm during their younger years and make it prosperous. Later each would be given a stake

to go into an occupation of their choosing. To provide
this stake, John would sell off a parcel of his land and
give the proceeds to the son in question. This is
evidenced by transactions recorded and kept by the
Lincoln County Registry of Deeds in Wiscasett.

All the sons chose to the leave the farm except for Moses.
Aaron became a shoemaker, John Adam and Cyrus
became merchants, Hector a house joiner, Henry a
carpenter and Washington a storekeeper. Upon his
death in 1845, John left what remained of his holdings to
his son Moses. The record clearly shows the chosen
work for each of the sons with the exception of Absalom,
born in 1806. By coincidence another Levensaler was
born that same year with name of Jacob. It may be that
this Jacob is really Absalom using his preferred name.
The lack of information about him remains one of the
curiosities of the family.

John died on February 14, 1845; his wife Katherine, died
two years later on September 16, 1847. Both are buried
in the Commery Cemetery in Waldoboro with their son,
Moses. Most of Johns' descendants stayed in New
England and live there today. Some settled in
Massachusetts and a few in New York State, but most
are still in Maine.

The following is a brief outline of two generations of
Johns' Waldoboro Levensalers with some pertinent
notations:

AARON

Aaron; John's first child was born on May 30,1801 in
Waldoboro. He married Mary Benner on January 1,1838
at a rather advanced age. Aaron work in Waldoboro
Village as a shoemaker. His shop was wiped-out by the
fire of 1846. Aaron died in July of 1872 and is probably

buried with his wife in the Commery cemetery. Aaron's children in birth order are as follows:

Webb
He was born in Waldoboro in 1838, there is no record of marriage or death.

Aaron
He was born in Waldoboro in 1840, there is no record of marriage or death.

Maria
She was born in Waldoboro in 1842, there is no record of marriage or death.

Washington
He was born in Waldoboro in 1844, there is no record of marriage or death.

MOSES W

Born in Waldoboro on February 22, 1804, Moses married Sally Hahn on December 13, 1832. He inherited the family farm in North Waldoboro and worked it for forty years. Moses died on March 29, 1882 and is buried with his wife and father and mother in the Commery Cemetery. His large family of nine children are listed in birth order as follows:

Catherine A.
She was born in Waldoboro in 1835 married Ezra Genther in January 22, 1855.

Nancy M.
She was born in Waldoboro in July 1836 and died in 1852.

Maria

She was born in Waldoboro in 1837. There is no record of marriage or death.

Warren

He was born in Waldoboro in 1838. There is no record of marriage or death.

William H.

He was born in Waldoboro in 1840, married Laura Cunningham on May 10,1862. He was mustered into the Union Army on August 29,1862, and was discharged on June 4,1865 at the end of the Civil War. He is listed on the army roster as a farmer, 21 years old, married, 5' 8 ¾" tall with blue eyes, light hair, and light complexion. After the War he married Lizzie Waltz on May 4,1867. He was listed as a charter member of the Kaizer Post of the G.A.R. He was one of the founders of the Medomak Mutual Fire Insurance Company in January of 1894. Member of the Board of Selectmen and a real estate agent. William Died on July 14,1919.

Mary A.

She was born in Waldoboro in 1842. There is no record of marriage or death.

Edward F.

He was born in Waldoboro in 1845. Edward married Jane B. Willett on October 5,1874. He served on the Board of Directors, Medomak Mutual Fire Insurance Co. He was elected to the Maine State Legislature in 1886. Eventually, retired to his farm in Waldoboro. Edward died on July 4,1919.

Moses W.

He was born in Waldoboro in 1848. Married Mary E.W. Miller on February 11, 1881. Moses was a

school principal and superintendent in the
Waldoboro school system. He was elected Town
Treasurer in the years 1883,1885,1897,1908. He
also organized the Waldoboro Water Company and
finally retired as a retail clothier. He died on
October 1,1914.

Roscoe 0.
He was born in Waldoboro in 1852 died six years
later in 1858.

ABSALOM

Born on June 27,1806 and died on October, 1882. There
is no record of marriage or children. He either left the
Waldoboro area or went by another name. There is a
Jacob Levensaler with approximately the same dates. It
could be that Jacob was Absalom preferred name.

MARY LEANORA

Mary was born in Waldoboro on March 8,1809. On
January 2, 1832 she married Edward Benner. The
record shows she died on November 26, 1858. Edward
was born in Waldoboro on June 7, 1799 and died on May
18, 1866. He is buried in the German Cemetery in
Waldoboro. There is no record of children.

JOHN ADAM

John A. Levenseller, the fourth son of John and
Katherine Levenseller was born on March 23, 1812. He
lived on his father's farm for twenty-seven years, until he
married a local woman, Elcey Benner on June 22, 1839.
Elcey was the daughter of Phillip Benner a neighbor and

a member of a family very closely associated with the
Levensalers. There are at least seven marriages between
the two families. The two families migrated to America at
the same time, on the same voyage in 1753.

John A. was fortunate in that he was starting his work-
life during the great days of expansion in Waldoboro.
The Town's shipbuilding industry and the resulting
commerce that was created were just coming into their
own and business was booming. He became a leader in
town and contributed greatly to the prosperity of the
time. It is probable that John was bilingual while his
father spoke mostly German, this helped him in his role
as arbitrator and adjudicator. When he married in 1839
he bought property from William Sproul and settled in
the village away from the family farm. From his start as
a mariner, he was later able to establish himself as a
merchant and trader. In his own self-interest, he became
a member of the first fire company formed in 1839. This
volunteer effort would be an omen of things to come.

In 1844, John was elected to the Board of Selectmen and
later in 1846 he listed as deputy sheriff. John was also a
Justice of Peace during these years. Legal documents in
existence today that are hand-written and signed by
John, are proof that he performed in this capacity. *(See
Appendix IV)*

In 1846, the records show that John and his brother,
Cyrus were burned out by the great fire that consumed
the entire business district of Waldoboro. John helped
rebuild the business but he later sold out to his brother
Cyrus in 1849.

Shipbuilding records researched by Stahl show that in
1850, John built an 82 ton schooner which he named
"Orbit" (see Appendix IV). This broad-beam schooner was
of the class called coasters. They were used to carry
cargo, (lumber and lime) up and down the East Coast.
Trips were made to as far north as Halifax, Nova Scotia

and as far south as Savannah, Georgia. The schooner *"Orbit"* put in four years of such service until April 18,1854; when she was wrecked in a storm off Point Alderton in Hull, Massachusetts. The schooner was lost and had no insurance, but the crew and cargo of lumber were saved. *(See appendix IV)*.

John continued in business, working with his brother Cyrus and at this time became an agent for the Mechanics Association of Waldoboro. On August 25, 1854, John and Cyrus' business was again wiped out by fire. This fire was so devastating that not a store, workshop, public house or office was left in town. As a result no provisions, clothes, furniture or medicine could be purchased. After two great fires in less than ten years, the town was rebuilt in brick. with the two disasters John suffered in 1854, it is surprising that he continued in business, but as late as 1860 he is listed as a merchant in Waldoboro.

After sixty-two years of struggle and enterprise, John left a rich legacy of achievement and determination. John died on August 23, 1874 leaving his wife, Elcy, to be a widow for thirty-two years until she died on December 28, 1906. Both are buried in the Commery Cemetery in Waldoboro with many other members of old German families. Although John was a business and civic leader, he raised rather ordinary children who did not distinguish themselves in any special way. The four boys and two girls would lead relatively uneventful lives, four of them would leave Waldoboro only to return before their last days. Johns' children are listed in birth order as follows:

Alonzo
> He was born in Waldoboro on August 15,1841. Married Mary E. Wharfinger from that town. Worked as a fisherman out of Rockport, Massachusetts.

Myron

He was born in Waldoboro on May 1,1842 and died before his first birthday on April 11,1843. He is buried in the family plot in the Commery Cemetery in Waldoboro.

Oris

He was born in Waldoboro on February 15,1844. Married Sarah Magune. Was a stonecutter in Waldoboro. Died in Waldoboro on September 3,1915 and is buried in the Commery Cemetery.

Azro

He was born in Waldoboro on September 10,1846. Married Mary Williamson from Glocester Massachusetts. His second marriage was to Emma Campbell of Nova Scotia. Azro was a fisherman, sailor, cook, painter, and Handyman in Waldoboro, ME., Rockport,MA., Providence, RI. He died on November 11,1922 and is buried in the Commery Cemetery in Waldoboro.

Susan A.

She was born in Waldoboro on July 24,1850. Married Murray F. Benner. Adopted Alonzo's boy Chester. Died in August of 1941.

Florance

She was born in Waldoboro on September 23,1857. Married Fredrick W.Folsom on September 23, 1874. Later married William J. Weeks on October 31, 1884. Died on April 3,1934 and buried in the Commery Cemetery with her second husband.

CYRUS

Born in Waldoboro on November 8,1814. Married a women named Margaret date unknown. He died on July

30, 1890. Worked as a ships carpenter and merchant in Waldoboro. They had two children:

Lewis K.
Born in Waldoboro in 1859, Married Leonora A. Day, died in 1950 and is buried in Waldoboro.

Ada B.
Born in 1864, Married Elmer E. Newbert, on July 4,1882.

HECTOR BROWN

Born in Waldoboro on April 12,1817. Married Louisa J. Genthner on September 19,1846. Died on November 15,1899. Worked as a house joiner in Waldoboro and lived near Robert Miller. They had two children:

Hudson
Born in Waldoboro on August of 1848. Died at a young age of 21 on December 19,1869

Hattie
Born in Waldoboro in 1851. Married Thomas Fitzgerald on February 28,1874.

HENRY

Born in Waldoboro on March 25,1820. Married Elizabeth Kaler. Henry joined the Union Army on August 22, 1862 and was assigned to Company A, 22nd Massachusetts Infantry. He saw action in the battle of Fair Oaks, Virginia where he was wounded in the hand. Later, during the Wilderness Campaign, he was mortally wounded at Laurel Hill, Virginia on May 8, 1864. He died in Fredericksburg on May 22, 1864. *(See Appendix IV)* Henry and Elizabeth had two children:

Alexis

He was born in Waldoboro in 1850 and later married a woman named Laura.

Laura A.

Lura was born in Waldoboro in 1853. There is no record of marriage or death.

HARRIET ALAMANDA

Harriet was born in Waldoboro on April 4, 1822. She married Sterling Davis on May 16, 1857. There is no record of death or burial.

WASHINGTON

Washington was born in Waldoboro on May 14, 1825. He died in February 11, 1843 at the age of eighteen

JOHN A. LEVENSELER

1812 - 1874

A CLOSER LOOK AT A BRANCH OF THE FAMILY

This section constitutes a further examination of the family of John A. Levensaler (1812 - 1874) and Elcy Benner (1816 - 1906).

ALONZO LEVENSALER

Alonzo Levensaler was born on August 15,1841 and was raised in Waldoboro. He married a girl from a local family, Mary E. Wharfinger then moved to Rockport, Massachusetts. He worked out of this seaport as a sailor and fisherman. While in Rockport, they had two children, Lizzie F., born January 22, 1870 and John A. born November 11,1874. Azro, Alonzos' brother eventually joined him in Rockport where they worked together as fishermen.

When his father died, Alonzo moved back to Waldoboro and lived in the father's home where he cared for his widowed mother. Here he continued to work as a fisherman and had a second son, Chester A. born in 1882. In 1900 Alonzo's oldest son, John A. was listed in the U. S. Census as a private in the U.S. Army, stationed in Portsmouth, Rhode Island.

The last record of Alonzo is in the 1906 town census, where he is listed as living in Waldoboro with his wife and mother. His youngest son, Chester, who would inherit the family property, was last recorded as living with his aunt Susan, who also lived in Waldoboro.

ORIS LEVENSALER

Oris Levensaler, third son of John A. and Elcy was born in Waldoboro, Maine on February 15, 1844. He seemingly spent most of his life in Waldoboro, learning the stonecutters trade at an early age. There is, however, a strong suspicion that he and his two brothers spent time at sea. There is no record of children from his marriage to Sarah Magune and not much is known about his personal life. Oris was married to Sarah on May 11, 1892 in Rockport, Maine. He did become proficient in his trade and an example of his craft is the stone that graces his sister Elcis' grave.

At mid-life he is listed as owning his own shop in the Town of Waldoboro and lived at 48 Jefferson St. Oris died on September 3, 1915 and is buried in the Commery Cemetery with his wife Sarah, who died in 1936. It is interesting to note, that he has an anchor on his gravestone which may indicate some connection with the sea that we do not know about.

AZRO LEVENSALER

Azro Levensaler, born on May 4, 1846 in Waldoboro, was the youngest of four boys, and he along with two younger sisters, made up the family of John A. and Elcy Levensaler.

At an early age, Azro turned to the sea for a livelihood. He became a deck hand and cook on coastal sail and steam ships. Two of the ships he sailed on were the "Heavener" and the "Roxmont". In his early twenties he moved to Rockport, MA. to work and live with his brother Alonzo. While living there he met and married a woman from nearby Gloucester, Massachusetts, Mary Ellen Williamson. Their first child, Mary Ellen, was born in Rockport in October, 1869.

Three years later, Azro and his brother Alonzo moved back to Waldoboro, where Azro's son, Walter Lincoln was born on January 18, 1873. During the next few years Azro continued to work at sea, until he was disabled after

being struck in the arm by a ships boom that came loose
in a storm. After this accident, he gave up the sea and
moved to Providence R.I., he is listed there in 1880 as a
house painter.

In 1898, Azro and Mary Ellen were separated and
divorced. Both their children had left home by that time;
their daughter had gone to school in Boston and was
living there, their son was married and living in
Waldoboro. Azro moved back to Waldoboro to live with
his son, while his divorced wife remarried on March 21,
1900 and settled in Rockport, Maine. There she set up
housekeeping with her new husband Charles Dexter
Wheeler.

Soon after arriving in Waldoboro, Azro took a second
wife, Emma Campbell a woman from Nova Scotia. They
were married on June 5, 1901 in Waldoboro. The town
report of 1902-1903 shows that Azro was doing work for
the town making school-house repairs and painting
bridges . In 1906 Azro's mother, Elcy, died. Soon
afterward he liquidated the property left by his mother,
including land around Storer's Wharf, where Azro's
father had built ships.

Azro spent his last days living in a small house at 201
Nobleboro Road in Waldoboro, where he kept a few farm
animals. He worked doing inside house repairs, painting
and wallpapering. He died on November 11, 1922 from a
stroke suffered while cleaning up debris his garden. He
is buried in the Commery Cemetery in a grave near his
father and brother Oris. Azro was the last of his line of
Levensalers to own property in Waldoboro

Azro was a member of a generation that began the
transition out of Waldoboro. He was not bilingual like
his father. He was taught in an English speaking school
system and was comfortable with his primary language.
He could take a non-German wife and could venture
outside Waldoboro for employment. His generation in

fact started a trend that continued from then on. During this time there was a shifting away from the old German ways in town. There was now a sharing of tradition and leadership with the English settlers. For the first time in the family history, he was not given the opportunity to follow in his fathers footsteps. Waldoboro had changed forever. These changes had a marked effect on Azro because in a real sense he was set adrift. Cutting ties with the old but not fully integrated with the new.

He eventually settled back where he was the most comfortable. His failed marriage and drifting provided a poor role model for his son and daughter and lead to further disintegration of the family. These dramatic changes caused the future generations to lose their identity and sense of family tradition. In spite of this legacy, Azros' four grandsons were able to bring a sense of family back to the fore with strong binds among them and with long faithful marriages.

AZRO LEVENSALER

1846 - 1922

SUSAN LEVENSALER

Susan was born in Waldoboro, on July 24, 1850. She spent her entire life in the Town and developed into a true citizen of Waldoboro like her father before her. On April 25, 1877, at the age of 26, she married a local man, Murray Benner, the son of Isaac Benner, a close friend of the family. There is no record of children from this marriage. Susan was reputed to be a small, slight woman standing under five feet tall with great energy. She was very busy in local affairs and interested in historical accounts of the first German families that settled in Maine. She is said to be the first Levensaler to trace the family roots back to Germany. Family lore has it that Susan and her sister Florance kept the family traditions and history alive in their memory. Unfortunately, there is no record that they ever reduced their knowledge to writing.

Data from the 1880 U.S. Census show that Susans' mother, Elcy, had moved in with them after her husband, John, had died. Later in the 1910 census Susan is listed as living at 50 Jefferson Street in Waldoboro with her husband and Alonzos' son Chester A. Levensaler, whom they eventually adopted.

Susan died in August of 1941 at the age of 91 and is buried with her husband in the Commery cemetery in Waldoboro. She probably had the most longevity in the family.

FLORANCE LEVENSALER

Florance was born in Waldoboro on September 23, 1857 and would spend most of her life in the town. On September 23, 1874, her birthday, she married a local

man, Fred W. Folsom. They had a daughter Lena, who
was born on August 20, 1878.

Lena would lived in Waldoboro all her life and marry three times.
First, to George H. Page, on April 5, 1899. Second, to Charles
Mcloon. Third, to a Benner on February 8, 1913. She had two
children by Charles Mcloon; Florence born in 1900 and James born
on January 26, 1905. There is no record of children from the other
two marriages. Lena died in August of 1941.

On October 31, 1884, Florance remarried, this time to
William J. Weeks. In 1910, they are listed a living at 186
Orf's Corner Rd. in Waldoboro. She moved to Taunton,
Massachusetts sometime after that but later moved
backed to Waldoboro. Florance and William had no
children of their own, but raised Florances' grandchild,
James Mcloon.

William died in July of 1929 and Florance five years later
on April 3, 1934 at he age of 77. James Mcloons'
daughter, Muriel, born on October 27, 1931, now is in
possession of the family Bible, as James died in October
of 1966. Florance is buried with her father, mother and
second husband in the Commery cemetery in Waldoboro.

MARY ELLEN LEVENSALER

Mary Ellen was born in Rockport, Massachusetts on
October 29, 1869 and was the first child of Azro and
Mary Ellen (Williamson). She started her public
schooling in Waldoboro but finished up in Providence,
Rhode.Island. After completing high school, she went to
work in Providence at the Davol Company. Later she
went on to business school in Boston taking a job as a
stenographer and settled down in that city. Sometime
before 1906, she married Arthur Beal, an established
pharmacist. Beal suffered from tuberculosis and was
told to move to a dryer climate. Returning from a visit to

Arizona, Beal died on the train. After his death Mary moved to her aunt Florance's house in Waldoboro.

Around 1900 she received a desk from her brother that was built from scrap lumber and old cigar boxes. This desk is one of the few heirlooms that have passed down from one generation to another. The desk stands as a memorial of Walter's craftsmanship as a cabinet-maker and devotion to his sister Mary.

Mary Ellen second marriage was to Dr. Benjamin Myers, a podiatrist, on Halloween, 1906 with the ceremony being held at her aunt's house. She survived him as well and like her aunt, Susan, remained childless through both marriages.

Dr. Myers was a member and officer in *"The Society of Redmen"*, Mary became a member of the woman's auxiliary of the society called *"Pocahontas"* and as her involvement grew she was selected to hold office in the club. As time went on, this activity became an important part of her life.

In the early forties Mary had the terrible experience of having a trolley car run over her while she was crossing Tremont Street in Boston. She survived this experience and lived to be 78. Mary died on May 10, 1948 and was buried on May 13, 1948 interred at #44 Birchdale (Section 1) with her husband Benjamin in the Woodlawn Cemetery in Malden.

The family speculated that Mary Ellen was left a sizable estate from her two affluent husbands. No evidence of this could be found upon her death; she left only some useless mining stock. If she ever had any wealth it was stolen away by unscrupulous investment counselors during her later years. She, like her brother was one step away from the poor house when she died.

WALTER LINCOLN LEVENSALER

Born in Waldoboro, Maine on January 18,1873, Walter
was the only son of Azro and Mary Ellen. In his early
years in Waldoboro he was able to exhibit his wood
working skills by building a canoe from scratch which he
sold for $12, a healthy sum in those days.
Unfortunately, Walter was brought up at a time when the
town was going from a boom to a bust. The shipbuilding
period was on the wane and the town began to be
eclipsed by other centers of commercial activity. This
would eventually force Walter look for job opportunities
elsewhere. At a young age he took to the sea like his
father before him and he became a captain of a two-
masted schooner out of Waldoboro. On January 1, 1895,
Walter married Lura Belle Merrifield from Hope, Maine.
They first settled in Rockport, Maine, later moved to
Waldoboro, then in 1902 to Portland, and in 1905 to
Everett, Massachusetts. During this time, Walter was
moving around to where he could find work. He was
employed as a ship's hand, ship's captain, shipwright
and carpenter. By 1912, Walter and Lura Belle had a
family of four boys and a girl, born in two different states
and four different towns:

Arthur E.	Born: June 20,1898 in Rockport, Maine
Raymond E.	Born: October 10,1899 in Waldoboro, Maine
Elcie M.	Born: 1902 in Portland, Maine
Leon W.	Born: July 13,1905 in Everett Massachusetts
Carl S.	Born: May 17,1912 in Everett, Massachusetts

In 1913 the family moved to a new house that Walter was
building in Dedham Massachusetts. This house still
stands today at 69 Berkley Road. Unfortunately, the
move to this house started a dark period in Walters' life
from which he would never fully recover. While working
to complete part of the roof he fell off and shattered his

elbow. He was admitted to Massachusetts General Hospital to repair his arm. After the operation, they administered alcohol to ease the pain, and he allegedly became addicted. With his drinking he began to experience financial setbacks and he eventually lost his equity in the house. His mood and temper changed; one day in a drunken rage he spread kerosene around the house and threatened to set it on fire. The police were called, but he sobered up enough so that he was not taken into custody.

After this episode, his wife, Lura was afraid to live in the house any longer and she packed up her possessions, moved out never to return. She eventually sought a and received a divorce. With her departure the family came apart, Arthur and Raymond drifted, picked up odd jobs and had to fend for them selves. At the outbreak of World War I Arthur joined the Canadian Army and Raymond joined the U.S. Navy. Leon went to Maine to live with his grandmother and Carl went with his mother. As a result of these occurrences, Walter suffered a severe nervous breakdown and was admitted to the Massachusetts Memorial Hospitals. He was later committed to the Westboro State Hospital for observation. After a period of recovery, he was released into the custody of his mother's second husband, Charles Dexter Wheeler, with the provision that he stay away from his ex-wife.

Walter moved to Camden, Maine with his mother and step-father. He took a job in the shipyard there, building and finishing the interior cabins of ships. One of the ships he worked on was a large five-mastered schooner called "The Blue Peter". This ship broke up and sank on its maiden voyage off the coast of South America. Some believe, that it was sunk by a German submarine that was operating in those waters at the time. Walter later moved to Portland, Maine where, as a government contractor, he worked on the high school that was being finished there. Still working for the government, he started work at the Fore River Shipyard in Quincy,

Massachusetts. There he was put in charge of crew of men that where doing finished carpentry work on ships that were being built for the war effort. Later, he was transferred to Waterbury, Connecticut where he worked on clock and instrument cabinets for ships.

When the country entered World War I, he was told that he would have to change his name if he were to continue to work for the Government. People with German sounding names could not be employed. Anti-German sentiment was running high in Waterbury as it was alleged that a German baker was putting ground glass in his bread. Walter then changed his last name to Evens dropping the "L" at the beginning and the "aler" at the end. Dropping letters was less expensive than adopting an entirely new name.

When the war ended, Walter changed his name back to Levensaler and returned to Boston. There he went to work for a contractor named McPhee. During this period (1919-1924), he worked on counters, cabinets and interiors in many of the retail establishments in and around Boston. He lived in Cambridge at first, then moved in with his sister, Mary, in Everett. Later they lived at several locations in Somerville: (Elmwood Street, Iverloo Street and Park Street). While living in Somerville he worked for the American Casket Company and later for Harvard College.

During The Great Depression his sons, Raymond and Arthur persuaded him to join them in New York City. They provided him funds to take over and run a gas station business, but instead he used the money to support his habit. He was sent back to Boston, were he took an apartment off Union Square in Somerville. After the depression, he move to Massachusetts Avenue in Boston, where he maintained a few rooming houses owned by a Priest, who wanted to remain anonymous. Walter gave up his car while living this area, never to drive again.

At the approach of World II, Walter moved into a rooming
house on Dartmouth Street in Boston across from his
sister Mary. In 1948, Walter fell down in his room and
fractured his hip. Meanwhile his sister had become ill
with pneumonia. Both were admitted to Boston City
Hospital at about the same time. Walter recovered from
his injury, but his sister died.

Later that year, his son, Leon, brought him out to
Waltham to live with him. The arrangement lasted only a
few months as Walter demanded to be returned to
Boston. A short while after his return, he fell off a steep
curb and broke his arm. He was admitted to Boston City
Hospital and when recovered, was placed in a nursing
home in Jamaica Plain. He died there on April 8, 1955,
his body was transported to Waldoboro, Maine where he
is buried with his father in the Commery Cemetery.

LURA BELL LEVENSALER (MERRIFIELD)

Lura Belle was born in April 29, 1876 on a farm in Hope
Maine. Her parents were children of English settlers
Samuel Merrifield and Eliza (Cotton) on her father's side
and Samuel and Cynthia (Metcalf) Crabtree on her
mothers, side. Lura's father Benjamin and mother
Louise (Crabtree) were born into these respective families
that probably migrated from Massachusetts in the early
1800's.

Lura had three brothers and a sister: Clarence M. born
in 1867, Ulyses G. (Ulie) born in 1869, Lindsey E. born in
1873, Louisa C. born in 1871

Lura met Captain Walter Levensaler and they married on
New Year's Eve 1895. From this point forward, Lura was
destined to travel from one place to another for several
years. The newly-weds set up housekeeping in Rockport,

Maine and on June 20, 1898, she gave birth to her first son, Arthur. He weighed only a pound and a half at birth, but, in spite of this, went to live for over ninety years. The next year, Lura was living in Waldoboro with her father-in-law, Azro and gave birth to her second son, Raymond.

Some time after the family moved to Portland where in 1902, she gave birth to her only daughter, Elcy. She only lived a year and is buried in the Commery Cemetery in Waldoboro.

After this tragedy, Walter gave up the sea and became a full-time carpenter and cabinet-maker. Following his trade, they moved to Everett, Massachusetts, where their third son, Leon, was born on July 13, 1905. While still living in Everett, she gave birth to her fourth and last child, Carl, on May 17, 1912.

At this time, Walter was building a house in Dedham, and moved his family in while it was still under construction. This caused great hardship for the small baby and mother as the house was yet to be centrally heated. In 1915, after a violent episode with her husband, she took her youngest child and move back to Maine into her sister Louises' house and subsequently filed for and received a divorce. The sisters established a restaurant in Camden, which flourished for a number of years. Lura remarried around this time to a Allen Mc Lain of Camden. The three of them ran the restaurant until they were evicted by their brother, so he could sell the building.

Rather than trying to establish a restaurant in a new location she gave it up and moved to Yonkers, New York with her youngest son, Carl. It was no coincidence that she moved into the same apartment building where her sons Arthur and Raymond were living. She lived there until January of 1943 when she died of complications resulting from pneumonia. It was felt that she could

have been saved had she received doses of the new
wonder sulfur drugs that had just been developed.
These drugs were not available to the civilian population
during the war years. She is remembered as a quiet,
unassuming lady who enjoyed cooking and conversation.
She had a special passion for whist and bingo parties.
She suffered at the hands of an unkind father and raging
first husband. Lura is buried in the Woodlawn Cemetery
in Yonkers, New York.

ARTHUR E. LEVENSALER

Arthur was born in Rockport, Maine on June 20, 1898.
And was the first child of Lura and Walter Levensaler.
Arthur had a very poor start in life. Born premature, he
weighed just over a pound. In 1898, before incubators,
very few babies survived at this weight. Fortunately for
Arthur, his grandmother, Mary Ellen Wheeler, was a
midwife and nurse. Some attributed other powers to her
as well. In any case, she nursed Arthur during this
critical time. She feed him rooster blood with an eye
dropper and kept him in a shoe box padded with cotton
behind the wood stove to keep him warm. This
treatment was quite successful, as Arthur grew up with a
healthy lust for life. Although he never grew to great
physical stature and could not father children, his
courage, enthusiasm and humor were unsurpassed.

Arthur was the first to leave the house in Dedham in
1914 when the family broke up. At the age of fifteen, he
hired on as a deck hand on a tramp steamer and traveled
around the world. When World War I broke out, he tried
to enlist in the United States Army, but was rejected
because of his height (under five feet). Undaunted, he
traveled to Canada and enlisted in the Canadian Army.
He was assigned to warehouse duty and never saw
action. After the war, on April 26, 1918, Arthur married
a Malden woman, Edith M. Ward. The ceremony took
place in Everett, Massachusetts and was presided over

by his uncle, Benjamin Myers and witnessed by his father. On his marriage certificate he is listed as a tire builder living at 30 Garden Street in Needham. Arthur later settled in New York City and took a job driving a commercial oil truck. He worked through the Great Depression in this way. He divorced Edith in the early twenties and married again, this time to Helen Cipe, a woman from Long Island.

In 1942, at the outset of World War II, Arthur moved out to San Francisco, California with his wife Helen. He left New York City with a model "A" Ford, $60 in his pocket and high hopes. He went to work for the Navy as a warehousemen in the United States Naval Supply Depot in Oakland. He eventually bought a house in San Francisco on Pope Street. During this period, Arthur spent his time taking meticulous care of his car, bowling and planning out his next trip. Arthur worked for the Navy until he retired in 1964 at the age of 66.

During his retirement years he never lost his desire to travel and made annual trips back to Maine to visit his brothers and cousins even though toward the end he had become quite feeble. During his last trip, he celebrated his ninetieth birthday in Camden, Maine. Near the end of his life, he wished to move to Maine and live out his last days, but his wife was too ill to take the change in climate. Arthur died of pneumonia while living in a retirement community of Leisure Town in Vacaville, California on June 23, 1989.

RAYMOND E. LEVENSALER

Raymond Levensaler was born in Waldoboro, Maine on October 10, 1899. In contrast to his older brother, Raymond grew to be over six feet tall and eventually became the bully of the family. When the family broke

up in 1914, he went on to New York City and worked odd
jobs to survive.

With the Country's active involvement in World War I, he
joined the United States Navy as a seaman. He shipped
out on a merchant vessel but soon took ill with influenza
and as a result spent much of his active duty time in a
hospital in Scotland. When he was discharged after the
war he returned to New York City and went to work for
New York Edison as a wire inspector.

In 1922, he started his new job, and married a woman
from New York, Sadie Keogh. Sadie is a cousin of the
movie actress Joan Blondell. During the second world
war, she had the misfortune of working in the Empire
State Building when a Army Air Force B-25 crashed into
the building several floors below. She suffered only from
the shock of the incident. Sadie and Ray did not have
any children at first, but on November 27, 1933, they
had a daughter, Lois. She was to be their only child.

During the forties, Ray twisted and broke his ankle while
reading a meter in a dark basement of a house in the
Harlem section of New York. He had the ankle repaired
by having a steel pin implanted to hold together the
damaged parts. He continued to work for ConEd until
1964 when he retired after 42 years of distinguished
service.

Rays' trophy self was crammed with bowling awards
attesting to his skill and interest in the game. He always
liked a good argument, and even though he was short on
formal education, he was long on life experience making
him a formidable adversary.

Shortly after his retirement, Raymond and Sadie sold
their house, left the Bronx and moved to Maine. They
bought a small house in Camden outright, so that they
could live comfortably on their pensions. He was later
joined by his sister-in-law, Anita Keogh and his
daughter, Lois and her children. When his wife died in

1980, Ray became despondent and eventually was moved into a private rest home in Union, Maine. There, he developed an interest in the teachings of the Bible, which helped him to make peace with himself. He lived in this home until his death on November 28, 1988. He is buried with his wife in the Oak Hill Cemetery in Camden, Maine.

LEON WALTER LEVENSALER

Leon (Jack) Levensaler was born in Everett, Massachusetts, on July 13, 1905, third son of Walter Lincoln and Lura (Merrifield).

He lived his early years in Everett with his mother and father going to the first few years of public grade school and growing up with his brothers, Raymond and Arthur. About 1912, the family moved to Dedham, Massachusetts to a house the father was building on Berkley Road. The house was still being completed at the time they moved in and Leon and his brothers helped complete the construction. After a period of extreme hardship, Leon's parents separated and eventually divorced. This caused the breakup of the family and Leon was sent to live with his grandmother, Mary Ellen Wheeler in Rockport Maine. Here he continued school, and worked part-time in his aunts' (Louise Dunbar) restaurant in Camden and later in the Thorndike Hotel in Thomaston. While in Rockport, he contracted influenza during the great epidemic of 1913 and nearly died. His grandmother, who was a self-taught nurse and mid-wife caused Leon to have a major hemorrhage that purged his lungs and saved his life. However, this episode left a scar on one of the lungs that later caused major difficulty. During his senior year of High School, Leon was forced to drop out, because his father stopped

sending support. He moved to Somerville,
Massachusetts with his father and aunt, Mary. He found
a full-time job to help support himself and as a result,
never completed his education. Leon later moved to
Waltham, Massachusetts with his father. He found work
in a commercial photographic laboratory that developed
and produced "black and white" snap-shots and
enlargements. This, as it turned out, would be his life
work.

Work became the dominant factor in Leon's life and
seemed to increase yearly. It entailed long hours during
the week and many times work on the weekends. With
experience, he became a supervisor and eventually a
foreman of one of the production departments in the
laboratory. At this time he started having people call him
"Jack" as he was never fond of his real first name. From
that time forward he was always known as *"Jack"* by the
people he worked and socialized with. At about this time
he felt secure enough to marry and start a family.

Leon was married on June 12, 1932 to Elizabeth Adreani
(Born: September 26, 1908) of East Boston.
They raised three children:

Walter Louis: Born on January 18, 1934 in
Somerville, MA.

Anita Lura: Born on September 27, 1939 in
Waltham, MA.

John Dexter: Born on August 15, 1945 in
Waltham, MA.

In 1947, after twenty-five years of service, Jack was laid
off when his job was eliminated as a result of an
efficiency study. With his severance pay and his saving
he began his own business in the basement of his home.
He had taken a few customers with him from his
previous employer and a few part-time employees that

use to work for him. Under extremely poor conditions, he began his own photographic laboratory. Later some of his business acquaintances showed an interest in backing him. With their help he expanded the business and formed a corporation. With the new capitalization and an increased sales effort the business quickly expanded and became a major competitive force in the industry. Leon was the only corporate officer that had photographic experience and he became the General Manager of the enterprise. He hired and trained all the production employees and ran the day-to-day operation of the laboratory. Its' reputation grew for high quality work and the business continued to expand. In 1949, the business moved to new quarters and took on a major new stockholder. The group of original stockholders were reorganized and new majority stockholder became president and chief executive officer. Leon was named chief operating officer. At this time the family moved into their own house for the first time, in Waltham in 1950, day of great celebration.

Over a period of the next ten years the business began to decline as color and instant photography took its toll on this all black-and white business. The business finally stopped operation in 1960. At this time, Leon went to work for a large color laboratory, and learn the color photography process. He worked there until the laboratory moved out of reasonable commuting distance. Leon decided that he had enough and never worked in photography again.

He did not have time for many hobbies, but he did collect stamps and became an avid gardener. At one time he developed a crossword puzzle that was published in a Boston newspaper.

After retirement, Leon took part-time jobs as a guard and janitor until 1972 when he stopped working altogether. During his later years, he traveled to Europe and around the country. He finally got to do some of the things that

he could not do while working in his all consuming job.
In his declining years, he was able to see his eight
grandchildren mature and become young adults. He had
two great grandchildren at the time of his death.

As he began his eighties, his heart started to give him
trouble until in 1991 he had to have a valve replacement.
The heart operation was a success but his lungs began to
fail. Leon died at The Waltham Hospital on September 4,
1992 at 4:45 P.M. from Fibrosis of the lungs. He is
buried in the Holy Cross Cemetery, in Malden,
Massachusetts.

CARL S. LEVENSALER

Carl was born in Everett, Massachusetts in 1912. When
still a baby, he moved to a house his father was building
in Dedham, Massachusetts. He lived there until 1915,
when he moved to Maine with his mother. He was raised
in Maine, going to school in Rockport and living close to
his mother's family, the Merrifields.

After graduation, he moved to New York City where he
joined his two brothers Arthur and Raymond. He found
work there in wholesale dry goods house selling fine
fabrics and cloth.

In 1942 he joined the U.S. Army Signal Corp and spent
the first part of the war in the Azores as a
Communication Specialist. After V-E Day, he was
transferred to Germany with the occupation forces.
During this time, he sent home boxes of souvenirs,
cameras and stamps.

In 1947, he returned to New York to his old job and
worked his way into a senior sales position. After he was
established, he married Minne Scipe, a woman from Long

Island and settled in with her family. They had two daughters, Patricia born in 1954 and Susan born in 1956.

He worked at the same firm for 30 years and retired in 1977. With his retirement money and savings, he bought a piece of land in Camden, Maine within view of Mt. Battie. Eventually his wife and children and in-laws joined him in Camden living in three separate structures. Carl spent his retirement years close to where he was raised, enjoying his quite surroundings away from the city. He took great pleasure in discovery and enjoyed history and philosophy.

In March of 1994, Carl died at the age of 82, the last of his generation of Levensalers. He is buried in the Commery Cemetery in Waldoboro with his father, Walter and his grandfather, Azro; neither of which he has much to do with in life, but couldn't be closer in death.

CHAPTER III

THE CHRISTOPH LEVENSELLER FAMILY

Few accounts of this branch of the family are noted in the history of Waldoboro. Knowledge we have of this family's existence comes from the original ships list and records transmitted to the town archives by the Old German Lutheran Church. The town records show that there was a Christoph Levenseller, who had four sons and two daughters. This record does not show Christopher's birth date nor does it show the name of his wife. Church records in Germany, however, show that he was born on January 1, 1744 in Alten Dietz, Hessen-Nassau, Germany.

There is a single mention of Christoph in the Waldoboro town history, stating that he was one of the founders of the Lutheran Reform Church organized in 1772. No other mention is made of Christoph or his wife in any way. Stahl, in his *History of Broad Bay*, has listed all his children as belonging to Johan Adam thus adding to the confusion. A clear version of the history of this branch of the family is still a work in progress.

This lack of history gives some support to the tradition that he and his wife returned to Germany sometime before 1790. Later records show, however, that three of Christoph's sons and three daughters continued to live here. His children ventured out of Waldoboro at an early age, settling in wilderness areas around what is now the towns of Lincolnville, Waldo and Searsmont, Maine. To evidence this, *Levenseller Pond* and *Levenseller Mountain* (elevation 1048') are located on State Highway 173 on the boarder of Lincolnville and Searsmont.

Relatives of these families eventually ventured even further out into the interior, to the Mount Katahdin area and settled in the towns of Atkinson, Bowerbank and Sebec, Maine. An 1882 map of this area shows that Peter

Levenseller occupied lot #5 in Bowerbank. Modern maps show that *Levensaller Hill* (elevation 724') is near *Long Bog* in the town of Bowerbank. These towns are located north of Dover-Foxcroft and Sebec Lake in Piscatagua County, Maine.

CHRISTOPHS' CHILDREN

PETER

First child of Christoph, was born on February 11, 1765 in Waldoboro. There is no record of marriage or death in the town archives.

MARI CATHARINE

First girl of the family, was born on December 8, 1766 in Waldoboro. Married George Schumann, possibly her cousin, on October 8, 1792 in Waldoboro.

JACOB

Jacob, the second son of Christopher was born in Waldoboro on September 8, 1768 (The Johan Levenseller family Bible shows his name to be John Jacob). As a young man, Jacob moved to nearby Camdentown and is shown there in the first U.S. Census as being a single, head-of-household *(see Appendix III)*. Five years later, the town records show that he married Hannah Jane Maropat Barter on July 25, 1795 in Camdentown. Jacob then moved to the Plantation of Ducktrap/Canaan (now Lincolnville), where in the next census (1800) he is listed with two daughters and a son. Jacob apparently died between 1800 and 1808 at a relatively young age. His widow remarried a John Norton on June 12, 1808. She died on October 3, 1874 at the age of 78yrs. 2mos. and

18days. She is buried in the Lower Cemetery in
Lincolnville. Three of Jacob and Hannas' children may
be:

Jacob Levensaler

Jacob was born in 1798 in Lincolnville, Maine. He
married Martha Parsons (born in 1800) on
November 23, 1826 in Montville, Maine. They
moved to Atkinson, Maine where Jacob developed
and managed a family farm. Here they raised a
large family of at least eight children that spread
far and wide across the United States. Jacob died
on March 15, 1870 and was survived by the
following children:

Joan	Born 1828	Jacob Jr.	Born 1830
Betsy	Born 1835	Moses	Born 1838
Martha	Born 1839	Leonard	Born 1842
Mary E.	Born 1845	Rose E.	Born 1850

Mary D.

Mary married a man named John Buzzell and had
children named Hannah and Hezekiah.

Hezekiah

Hezekiah was born in Lincolnville in 1801. In 1829,
Hezekiah married Margaret Dean. She was from
the local area and was older than Hezekiah being
born in 1799. They settled Lincolnville and raised a
family of four children:

Margaret A.

She was born in Lincolnville in 1835

Francis H. (Frank)

Was born on October 26, 1837. He married
Jennie Luce and settled in Lincolnville, Maine
that today is the site of *"Levenseller Mountain
and Levneseller Pond"*. Their son, John
Wesley was born on January 8, 1870. Jennie
died two years later on February 7, 1872.

Francis then married his wife's cousin, Cynthia Luce. They in turn, had three children: Addie P., born on June 8, 1873, Edgar Frank, born in June of 1876 and Jennie Marie born on June 2, 1877. Cynthia died on April 9, 1910 and was buried in Oak Grove Cemetery in Searsmont. Francis died on June 26, 1911 and is buried in Searsmont. Francis rose to prominence in town as a town selectmen, town clerk and superintendent of schools. There is further record showing the their daughter Jennie Marie married John Wilber Morse and that she died in Belfast on July 9, 1907. Their children were Hazel, born on October 13, 1898 in Belmont, Maine. She died in Belfast in October of 1970. Their second child; Bertha Morse married Roscoe Dean.

Samuel A.
He was born in Lincolnville in 1839.

Frank
He was born in Lincolnville in 1855 and married Mary E. Woods. Frank and Mary had two boys: Charles born in 1874 and Judson born in 1878.

GODFREY

Christoph's third son, Godfrey, born on May 13,1769, stayed in Waldoboro all his life, probably on the original homestead. He married a woman from a Waldoboro family, Christiania Snowdeal, daughter of William, on January 22, 1793 and raised a family of three sons and four daughters. The identity of these children is not clear. Godfrey was not active in Town events and is not mentioned in the town history. However, records of old invoices do show that he was a blacksmith as well as a farmer and he proved services for the farmers living around him. He died around 1855 at the age of 85, but there is no public record of where he is buried.

Peter Levenuller

Peter appears in the 1840 Census that could be one of Godfrey's sons. He is shown to be living in Bowerbank, Maine, Piscatqua County. He was born in 1794 and his wife Betsy in 1805. They raised a very large family on their farm and never left his settlement. Peter is undoubtedly one of the early settlers in Bowerbank as there is a hill in that town named after him. This clan, located in an isolated, interior part of Maine, began spelling their name in a unique fashion; perhaps to distinguish themselves from other Levensellers or perhaps to spell the name phonetically to reduce the number of mispronunciations. They spell the name "LEVENSAILOR". There are still, a number of families that spell their name this way. Peter and Betsys' surviving children were:

Thomas	Born in 1824	Peter	Born in 1834
Joseph	Born in 1827	John	Born in 1838
Sally	Born in 1831	Debra	Born in 1841
Silas	Born in 1832		

CHRISTOPHER (STEPHEN)

The Fifth child of the family, Christopher was born: (Stephen) August 26, 1771 in Waldoboro. In the 1790 U.S. Census he is listed as a soldier living Boston. Married Jemimah Young on December 18, 1795 in Camdentown. Jemimah was the daughter of Gideon and Jemimah (Cilley) Young and she had a brother Moses. Stephen is listed in the U.S. Census of 1800 as living in the plantation of Ducktrap/Canaan with three sons and a daughter. Stephen died in Belfast Maine in 1807. His widow Jemimah, remarried in 1812 to an Andrew Peirson. It is possible that two of Stephen's three sons were:

John K.
Born on May 21 1807 in Waldoboro and died June 8, 1868 in Waldo. He married Sarah Gay who was born on April 18, 1824 in Union, Maine and died on June 8, 1907 in Waldo. John had three children:

Gilbert	born 1850,
Charles	born 1855
John M.	born 1860.

Leonard M.
Born in 1802 may be Christopher's second son. Leonard lived with his wife, Evaline, born in 1809 in Waldo, Maine their daughter Rebecca, born in 1831 and their son John W. born in 1848.

BATTY (ELIZABETH)

Christophers, sixth child was born on May 26, 1773 in Waldoboro. She married Andrew Hoffses on February 23, 1799. She moved and settled in Warren, Maine, where she died on July 18, 1872. She is buried in the Stahl Cemetery in Warren. There is no record of children at this time.

SALLY

Sally, the last child born into the Christopher family. She was born around 1796 in Waldoboro. On November 12, 1818 she married William Schwatz also of Waldoboro. There is no record of children, death or burial.

CHAPTER IV

THE ANNA MARGARETHA FAMILY

Anna Margaretha the sixth and youngest child of Pieter and Anna Margaretha Lievenzöllner and younger sister of Johan Adam and Christop, was married on January 31, 1768 at the New South Church in Boston to Philip Johann Peter Hilt. Peter is reputed to be one of the patriots that dumped tea into the harbor in 1773. After their marriage they moved to a new settlement which later became Hope, Maine. In A. S. Hardys' *"History of Hope"* she relates the following bit of history:

Philip Hilt, the father, drowned in the Pond (Canaan) after the close of the Revolution. It could have been as late as 1785. The widow Margaret (Lievenzollner) and the children remained at their site in the wilderness, the older boys enlarging the clearing for crops and Margaret and Betsey spinning and weaving to help sustain the family. Betsey would later marry Abner Heal, a neighbor across the pond in Lincolnville. In 1786 Margaret Hilt's lot became # 108 on the plan of Hope and she received her deed for the total lot in April of 1789. Her eldest son, John Hilt, now of age, took lot # 107 next to her. Their early cabins were on the hill overlooking the Megunticook Mountains and the lake where Earle Pearse Dairy Farm is now located. The original road from Camden came by Margaret's house, past the Hewitt lot and on to McLains' Mills, now Appleton Village.

Later records show that she may have died in Boston. The connection that both Johan and Margaretha had with Boston is not clear at this writing.

ANNA MARGARETHAS' CHILDREN

Johan
Johan was born on November 20, 1764 in Rutland, Massachusetts, married Lydia T. in 1791. Died on April 27, 1838 in Hope, Maine.

Peter
Born in 1771 in Hope, Maine. There is no record of marriage or death.

Elizabeth
Also known as Betsy, was born in 1773 in Hope, Maine. She married Abner Heal of Hope in 1793. Died in Hope, Maine.

William
Born in May of 1777 in Hope, Maine. Married Rhoda in 1799. Died on April 6, 1868 in Hope, Maine.

Philip
Last of the Hilt children, was born in 1777 in Hope, Maine. There is no record of marriage or death.

CHAPTER V

SOME LOOSE ENDS

There exist a number of conflicts in the various accounts of family relationships. This is caused in part by the inability to track family lines in the historical records that have survived through time. For example, there is a matter of dispute involving the records I have received from "Will" Whitaker of Murray, Utah and from Stahl's *"History of Broad Bay"*. Both sources attribute all the surviving second generation Levensaler sons to Johann Adam Levenzeler. Their records show that John Adam had a son John Jacob, born November 8, 1768 and a son John Godfrey, born; January 30, 1775. They claimed that it is not unusual to have two sons named John in German families and that the original family bible shows this to be a fact.

I believe that these are Christopher's sons instead. Church records transferred to the Town of Waldoboro show that Christopher's son Jacob was born on September 8, 1768 and Godfrey was born on May 13, 1769. If I am correct this would make Godfrey 24 years old when he married Christiniana Snowdeal. He would only be 18, if he were John Adam's son. Twenty-four is a more likely age for marriage in this time period. Following Witakers' genealogy chart further we find that John Godfrey married a Katherine Achorn six years after his first marriage to Christinana.

I dispute this assumption for in the 1850 United States Census, John Godfrey is listed as being 80 years old; this age coincides with Christophers' Godfrey not John Adams' who would be five years younger. Secondly, Godfrey is listed with his wife Christiana not Katherine. Looking in the Commery Cemetery, where John Godfrey is supposedly buried we find that there is a John Levensaler and his wife Katherine buried with their son

Moses and family. There is no trace of Christiana in the cemetery.

John Jacob's record of birth in the family Bible held by Atwood Levensaler shows John Jacob on a separate page and not in the birth order with the other children. Atwood agrees that Jacob is probable a nephew and not a son of John Adam. The other interesting fact is that John Jacob's birth date matches that of Christopher's son except for the month which is only two months off. The month of birth could easily be entered as an approximation.

Because of the way information was recorded in the United States Census from 1790 to 1840, a whole generation of Levensalers cannot be identified with their parents. During those years only the name of the head of the household was recorded, others in the household were identified by age, category and gender. Even the wife was not identified. Other sources such as family Bibles, gravestones, church and town records will have to be research to make the connections.

The parents for the following Levensalers have not been identified at this writing:

JOEL S. LEVENSELER

Joel was born in 1811, lived in Thomaston, Maine. Married Susan D. Healy, on October 4, 1833. He was a marble worker in Thomaston and an apprentice to the famous craftsmen, Sullivan Dwight. In October of 1851 he prepared a block of dark marble which was sent to Washington D.C. to be incorporated into the Washington Monument. Inscribed on the stone: *"From The Home of Knox, By the Citizens of Thomaston, Maine"*. Joel and Susan had three children.

Dodge H.
Dodge was born in Thomaston on May 15, 1836. He married Bertha Hall on November 11, 1858 and resided in Thomaston as mason. They had one child named Caroline F. born about 1859.

Winfield
Winfield was born on April 8, 1839 and died on October 3, 1843.

Mary Elizabeth
Mary was born on --- 23, 1841 and resided in Thomaston.

GEORGE V. LEVENSELLER

George was born around 1806, in Holden, Maine where he later married Nancy Rowe. They lived in a Brewer, Maine for a time but had their Son, Leonard E., who was born in 1848, in Holden. Their son married Eliza J. Robinson on December 24, 1868 in Bangor. Eliza was the daughter of Samuel Robinson and Mary Wright. Leonard died on May 9, 1911. George died on January 27, 1881.

JACOB LEVENSALER

Jacob was born in Waldoboro in 1808. He resided there with his wife Caroline who was born the same year as Jacob. They had three children:

Harriet A.
Born 1837

Mary A.
Born 1842

Elijah S.

Born in 1844. Enlisted in the Union Army as part of the 20th Maine Regiment. Listed on the roster as a farmer, 18 years old 5' 7" tall, gray eyed, brown hair, light complexion, single.

CHARLES L. LEVENSALER

Charles was born in 1828. He lived in Waldoboro, Maine with his wife Esther M., who was born in 1829.

JOHN D. LEAVENSALER JR. (III)

John was born in Waldoboro in 1812. He settled and lived in Washington, Maine with his wife Dorothy (Mink or Mank). Dorothy was born in Waldoboro in 1812 and died on January 28, 1891. John died on the same date nine years before in 1882. They had a very large family of eleven children

Thomas	Born 1834	Warren	Born 1845
James	Born 1836	Sarah	Born 1847
Mary J.	Born 1838	Emily	Born 1849
Susan	Born 1840	Alice	Born 1850
Lucy	Born 1842	Abba	Born 1851
Aldana	Born 1852.	Married Levi Pitcher on July 11, 1880 Died on July 19, 1916	

MORAPAT LEVANSELLER

Born in 1772 and lived in Camden, Maine.

JENNA A. LEVENSELLER

Born in 1821 and lived in Boston, Massachusetts.

AUSTIN LEVANSELEAR

Born in1823 and lived in Boston, Massachusetts. Wifes' name was Mary E. and was born in 1825. They had a child named Frank E. born in 1850.

RESULTS OF A SURVEY

In an attempt to gather additional information on the relationships among families, I decided to survey all the living Levensalers that I could find. In August of 1997, I took a listing of Levensalers from the telephone directory on the World Wide Web. I found eighty-five different households listed. There were five variations in the spelling of the name and they were located in nineteen different states. There were heavy concentrations of Levensalers in three states: Maine, New York and Texas.

I was disappointed in the response I received from my survey letter, but not surprised. Of the sixty-four letters actually sent out, four were return because of bad addresses, therefore I was dealing with sixty contacts. From the sixty contacts I received seven phone calls and four letters. The phone calls were from Washington State, Tennessee, New York State, California, Maine and Massachusetts. All were curious about my work but no one had any information about the Levensalers in the distant past; most could only go back as far as their grandfather. As a result, I was not able to tie any father-son relationships together.

All of the callers wanted to receive further information and showed interest in my project. The callers with the "Levensailor" spelling doubted that they were related to the other Levensalers. They also mentioned that they had a tradition of being lumbermen and loggers and that their families had left Maine many years ago, and wished never to return. One caller with this spelling claimed he was Scottish. Another person said that he had information about the family but he had to check with a woman who was writing a book because he did not want to preempt her work. Most callers promised to contact other family members and send me information on their branch of the family. At this writing I have received nothing from them. However, I do think that this is a step that had to be taken in the continuation of my family research. Upon reflection, I think that most of the phone calls I received were made merely out of curiosity.

Even with the sparse offerings, I was able to glean some information from the survey. The group of Levensalers still living around Waldoboro are all members of the same extended family probably belonging to Moses. In the larger clans such as the Levensailors, disputes and resentment have built up over the years so that these family members are not communicating with one another.

Judging from the response I received, the majority of the people I contacted have no concern or interest in the family history. A person conducting a survey such as this should be prepared to share much more information then they receive. There is also a sense that direct family information is precious and should be guarded. Although it has not advanced the effort of compiling a history, it has never-the-less, been beneficial. Just to become aware of the number and location of the families is an accomplishment. The variety of spellings that have survived and the various misconceptions of where the name came from is very revealing.

The letters I received were short and yielded very little information about old family connections. There are some interesting points however:

In a letter received from Gerald Levenseller in Tacoma, Washington, he connects all the Levensellers living in that state with the Levensellers that lived in the Searmont/Lincolnville area of Maine. He had traced his line back to Edgar Levenseller who in turn was the son of Francis and grandson of Hezekiah.

In a letter from Randall Levensaler in Oakland, California, he eludes to the fact that there may be a connection between the Levensalers and Ansel Adams the world famous photographer. Randalls' fathers name was Joseph and a relative of Captain Caleb of Thomaston one of Adam Levensalers' children.

There continues to be a need to research the Levensaler family as it existed in the mid-nineteenth century. As more and more genealogical data is retrieved and entered on the record for all to discover, we will be able to fill in the gaps.

APPENDIX I

TRANSLATION

OF

GENERAL WALDO'S CIRCULAR --- 1753;

WITH

AN INTRODUCTION BY JOHN L. LOCKE,

OF BELFAST

GENERAL WALDO'S CIRCULAR

After the treaty of Utrecht, a difficulty arose which threatened the extinguishment of the claims of the Thirty Proprietors, by which they were induced to engage the services of Brig. General Samuel Waldo, to effect an adjustment of the case. Proceeding to England, Waldo succeeded, by untiring application at court, in accomplishing the object of his mission. On his return, the Thirty Proprietors joined in surrendering to him, for his services, one half of the patent.

In 1732, Waldo caused his portion to be set off in severalty, and in the following year made extensive preparations for settlement. The first settlement was commenced on the St. George's River, during the year 1736, and consisted principally of Scotch-Irish people.

During his visits in Europe, Waldo had not been inactive in circulating proclamations holding forth to emigrants the most inviting offers to occupy the lands of his patent. In 1740, forty German families were induced by the representations of these circulars to accept of his offers. On their arrival they located at Broad Bay, and there laid the foundation of the present town of Waldoborouogh.

In 1753, General Waldo's son, Samuel Waldo, visited Germany for the purpose of furthering his father's schemes, and to that end issued and distributed the circulars now under consideration. The inducements herein set forth had the effect of inducing sixty families to emigrate.

*"Leaving their native homes," says Mr. Eaton, in his **Annals of Warren**, "they passed more than twenty miles by land, embarked in small boats upon the Rhine, descended that river to Dusseldorf, where they remained awhile for others to arrive, and then proceeded to Amsterdam. Embarking on board ship, they left that city, but touched at Cowes. Here several of their number died. From Cowes they sailed to Portsmouth, and thence to St.*

INTRODUCTION

George's River. At Pleasant Point they were transferred to a sloop, which they filled as close as they could stand, and were carried round to Broad Bay. They arrived there in September. Some were crowded into a house; some were disposed of among other settlers; and the remainder, far the greatest number, were put in a shed. This shed was sixty feet long, without chimneys, and utterly unfit for habitation; yet here these destitute exiles, neglected by their patron, whose promises in this instance, either from his absence or other cause, were wholly unfulfilled, dragged out a winter of almost inconceivable suffering. Many froze to death, and many perished with hunger or diseases induced by their privations. The old settlers were too poorly supplied themselves to afford much assistance to the new comers, who were fain to work for a quart of buttermilk a day; and considered it quite a boon when they could gain a quart of meal for a day's labor."

In the following spring Waldo appointed an agent, Charles Leistner, "to dispose of emigrants and deal out the provisions provided for them."

It is not here necessary to trace further the history of these pioneers. The hardships and suffering they underwent, and the wrongs they endured, will become matters of record for the future historian of Waldoborough.

Belfast, June 2nd, 1859.

GENERAL WALDO'S CIRCULAR

Continuation of collected advices and regulations relating to the lately settled Massachusetts, and particularly to Broad Bay and Germantown in New England.

[Extract from the Imperial Post newspaper, number forty seven, March 23, 1753.]

The Royal British Captain Waldo, hereditary lord of Broad Bay, Massachusettes, having arrived in Germany from New England, and having taken up his abode in the dwelling of Hofrath Luther, this is made known to all those who intend to go to New England this spring, and are seeking permission from their respective governments, and who further are able to pay the passage money, to the end that they may apply either to himself, or to these already made known places of address, viz: Luther's type foundry, and the office of Eichenberg's newspaper in Frankfort, Leucht and Allerger's printing office in Augsburg, Mr. John Lewis Martin (merchant) in Hilbroun, and Mr. Goethel's printing office in Spires, (all of which are hereby made known to be regularly authorized, where, also, any other information may be obtained), and learn what is absolutely certain in regard to their journey, and make their contracts; while at the same time there is not the slightest notice to be taken of those people who go about, sending back and forth, and undertaking that for which they have no authority; although much may be undertaken in the name of New England, and the people stirred up by those who have not received the slightest commission therefor. Accordingly, all other persons beside the above fully empowered houses, even if they profess to treat in the name of Samuel Waldo, Brigadier General in royal army of Great Britain; or pretend to do business for the advantage of his colony, where most of the Germans have settled; and if even American letters have already passed through their hands, and they have had some useless business transactions with men, ships, &c., not in the appointed places; or produce other sealed documents, attested of little worth, which savor of the old custom; all such persons, in so far as they have received no orders from the aforesaid houses, will be shut out from all concern in the matter. But at the same time, by virtue of the full power of attorney situated at Frankfort, all and everything will be considered as binding, which may be done by the highly esteemed son of this gentleman, the hereditary Lord of Broad Bay, or by the aforesaid full empowered houses.

The promised one hundred and twenty acres, German measure, will be measured out to each, as his own property, and that of his heirs in the same manner as if General Waldo himself had transacted the business, and had been personally present. While, then, the people are warned to apply no where else than at the aforesaid places, and not to undertake the journey at once, without special papers of assignment and acceptance, (which every man in the neighborhood must obtain and thus secure himself) and thus be sure of free passage; Because it is intended to take only a suitable number of those who can pay their in entire passage, or at least half of it (as in the case of some), and not all, as affirmed in the excitement got up here and there, by certain utterly unauthorized persons, in the name of New England, about which we hear of the greatest indignation being produced at the same time it is intended to oppose all fraud, to treat the people justly, and to confer a heritage on those who pay the whole passage money, on which no unfair demands will be made, as has been the evil custom; but what is for their advantage will be pointed out to those who are emigrating.

The time of departure, and the place of gathering, with and further information, will be made known to all.

To this it is now added that the passes already made out for this purpose in the name of His Britannic Majesty, by the Duke of New Castle, Secretary of State, together with the needed documents connected with it, also the suitable letters of recommendation to his excellency, Onslow Burrish, the Royal Minister at the honorable States Assembly at Ratisbon, are already given out.

FRANKFORT ON THE MAINE, MARCH 23, 1753

The substance, in brief, of the principal circumstances and conditions respecting the settlement of foreign Protestants, in the Province of Massachusetts Bay in New England, especially Broad Bay.

This province lies, and extends itself in breadth along the Atlantic Ocean, in general, east-north-east and south-south-west, from forty-one degrees to forty-three degrees north, and five hours west, according to the meridian of London. Its land is made up of great districts, or divisions, which belong to the government itself, or to the most prominent settlers, or to gentlemen residing in England, to whom it has been transferred by the crown, as Pennsylvania; therefore the economy or form of government rests upon almost the same basis as that; except that each of these districts can make certain domestic arrangements without depending on the General Assembly therefor, which otherwise might not be accomplished.

Boston, the principal city of this Province, which has been already built more than one hundred and fifty years, and is occupied by a great number of English inhabitants, in good circumstances, lies about midway between Philadelphia and Halifax in Nova Scotia. It is distant from this last named Province about five hundred English miles, and separated from it by a great bay called the Bay of Fundy. The climate is acknowledged to be healthy, and the soil is exceedingly fruitful, since the wood which grows there is mostly oak, beach, ash, maple, and the like, and it yields all manner of fruit as in Germany, but hemp and flax in greater perfection. Also, there is game in the woods, and many fish in the streams, and every one is permitted to hunt and fish.

The government of Boston, from whence is a well built road and regulated mail to go to Pennsylvania, which lies only sixty-five or seventy German miles from it, has lately, in an assembly held November 23d, 1749, granted to the foreigners, for a beginning in its Province, four townships, each more than twenty thousand acres (German) in extent, where they can settle. Since, shortly after, a ship full of Germans arrived from Philadelphia, and announced that some hundred families would follow them, and other property holders in the same Province followed their example, and granted a great part of their lands on similar conditions; in particular his Britannic Majesty's Brigadier General Samuel Waldo, on these considerations, viz: ___

No. 1   That those who will of their own accord, and with the permission of their government, settle in Broad Bay, shall dwell together in certain divisions, consisting of one hundred and twenty. In every such district there shall be given to the church two hundred acres; to the first preacher settling among them two hundred; to the school, two hundred; and to each of the one hundred and twenty families, one hundred acres, equal to more than one hundred and twenty German acres. And this land, provided they dwell upon it seven whole years, either in person or through a substitute, shall be guaranteed to them, their heirs and assigns forever; without having to make the slightest recompense, or pay any interest for it. Unmarried persons to twenty-one years and upwards, who permit themselves to be transported hither, and venture to build on their land, shall also receive one hundred acres, and be regarded as a family.

No. 2   All such foreigners, provided they are Protestants, so soon as they arrive in New England, like all other subjects of his Britannic Majesty, will enjoy the protection of the laws; will be authorized, so soon as the one hundred and twenty families are together, to send a deputy to the General Court to represent them; will be obliged neither to bear arms nor carry on war; in case war should arise, they will be protected by the government; and the free exercise of all Protestant religions will be granted them. On the other hand, the government aforesaid demands nothing further than that every one hundred and twenty families shall call and support a learned Protestant minister within five years, reckoning from the time of the grant.

No. 3 There shall be given to the colonists on their arrival necessary support for from four to six months, according as they arrive early or late in the season. But only those will have the advantage of this who shall go thither under the direction of the places of address aforesaid.

No. 4 And if one or two Protestant preachers, provided with good testimonials from the consistories and church meetings, and unmarried, whose care is the salvation of souls, should resolve to trust to Providence and the good will of Samuel Waldo, and go forth immediately, at the beginning, with the rest, they shall receive besides their free passage a little supply of fifteen pounds sterling, for two years, out of the above named capital. Also, it is hoped that their congregations will also do something in addition. Boards for the first church which is to be built shall be given, and delivered to them. It is further remarked that the first families going thither, although there should be several hundred of them, can all select their residences either in a seaport or on navigable rivers, where they can cut wood into cords for burning, or into timber for building material, and convey it to the shore, where it will always be taken of them by the ships for ready money, and carried to Boston or other cities, and from thence whatever they need will be brought back in return, at a reasonable rate. By means of which the people are not only able at once to support themselves until land is fit for cultivation, but also are freed from the trouble and expense of making wagons, and traveling by land, to which difficulties it is well known Pennsylvania is subjected. Also, the government aforesaid has heard from people themselves, who have already come from Pennsylvania itself, the unjust treatment (well known to the

world without and such announcement) which befel them
upon the sea, after they had sailed from Holland, and has
already made a regulation to prevent the like, for the future, in
the voyage from Holland to Boston; according to which, not
only the ship captains who bring the people over, but those
who accompany them, must govern their conduct by the
prescribed regulations, otherwise they will receive
punishment, and be compelled to give the people satisfaction;
and also the ship itself will be taken care of. Thus are the like
mischances in various ways prevented, and every one is made
secure.

In order to avoid prolixity, this is suffered to suffice. Any
one can easily gather out of what has been said, that it has not
been the intention to persuade people to this expedition; and
those who without this had resolved upon it of their own
accord, will try their best not to suffer themselves to be
deceived; and thus can, unhindered, carry out their journey in
the name of God, upon the next time announced to the public,
with governmental passports. He who in addition to this,
wishes to inform himself more definitely with regard to any
point, can apply to the houses and places of address made
known in the Imperial Mail newspaper of March 23, 1753, or
by prepaid letters.

We, Thomas Holles, Duke of Newcastle, Count L. S. Of Clare, Lord of Houghton, Baron Pelham, of Laughton, Knight of the Royal Order of the Garter, member of his Majesty's Secret Council, and first Secretary of State, &c.

To all Admirals, Captains, Officers, Governors, Mayors, Sheriffs, Justices of the Peace, Commanders, Custom House Officers, Overseers, Inspectors, and all others whom this pass may concern, greeting: This passport, made out in the name of the King, goes forth to desire, and demand of you, that you allow and permit the bearer of this pass, General Samuel Waldo, one of the principal Proprietaries in the part of the King's lands which lies on Massachusetts Bay, New England, together with his servants, his effects and whatever is needful to him, to travel free and unhindered from hence to Harwich, or to any other seaport in England, that he may there embark and pass over to Holland. Further, also, we hereby pray and desire, that all servants, officers, and subjects of all Princes and States, who are allied with, and friendly to the King, will permit the said General Waldo to pursue his journey to Frankfort on the Maine, or to any other place in Germany or in Switzerland, with the permission of the several Princes and States whom this may concern, in order to collect the people of the Protestant faith, who may wish to settle in the aforesaid Province of Massachusetts Bay. And further, in accordance with this, to permit him, the aforesaid General Samuel Waldo, and also such persons as in the aforesaid manner shall suffer themselves to be united with him, to travel, together with their guides and all their effects, free and unhindered, through Switzerland and the various countries of Germany toHolland, in order to embark at Amsterdam, or any other seaport of this country, to be transported to the aforesaid Province of Massachusetts Bay. Finally, all the King's servants who may chance to be in any territory of the aforesaid Princes and States, are hereby besought to support and to protect the aforesaid General Samuel Waldo in his purpose, so that he may easily carry out his plans aforesaid, and put them into effect.

Given at Whitehall, the second day of March, 1753, in the twenty-sixth year of the King's reign.

APPENDIX II

GERMAN DEPARTURE LIST OF THE
ELISABETH - 1753

The ship *Elisabeth,* Captain Pendock Neale, arrived in Broad Bay, Maine in the week prior to 18 October 1753. The exact arrival date is not yet known; the 18 October 1753 issue of the *Boston Newsletter* says that the ship *Elisabeth* had arrived at St. Georges at the eastward with about 400 Germans. An arrival date of about October 8th-10th seems likely.

The German departure list of the ship Elisabeth is taken from the Henry Knox Papers, New England Historic Genealogical Society, at the Massachusetts Historical Society, 50:124.

GERMAN DEPARTURE LIST OF THE
ELISABETH - 1753

1753 Specification der jenigen Colonnisten welche mit dem Schiff Elisabeth
Capitain Pendock Neale nach der Broad Bay gesandt worden.

Personnen [people]		Frachten [Freights]	Zahlt [paid]	restirt [unpaid]
6 Martin Ullmer		4	—	30
seine Frau				
tochter Rosina	alt 14 Jahr			
dito Elisabeth Catherina	12			
dito Jacobina	6			
dito Maria Margareta	2			
5 Godtfried Feyler von Eßelbrun		3	22 ½	—
seine Frau				
Töchergen	alt 8 Jahr			
Söhngen	4			
Tochtergen	2			
1 Casper Feyler von Eßelbrun		1	1 ½	6
5 Hanß Georg Leicht von ditto		3	18	4 ½
seine Frau				
Sohn Hanß Georg	10 Jahr			
Tochter Regina Catherina	4			
Sohn Peter	1 1/4			
7 Johannes Kintzel von Königsbach		5	22 ½	15
seine Frau				
Sohn Friedrich	16 Jahr			
Tochter Christina	13			
Sohn Bernhardt	12			
Tochter Margret	8			
dito Elisabet	6			
4 Martin Hoch		2 ½	—	18 3/4
seine Frau				
Sohn Hanß Georg	5 Jahr			
ditto Conrad	1			
3 Hanß Gorg Glaugenauer		2	—	15
seine Frau				
Sohn Jacob Friederich	1 ½ Jahr			
2 Johann Michael Heußler		2	—	15
seine Frau				
1 Salomon Rotner	20 Jahr1	1	—	7 ½
1 Felix Rotnner	18	1	—	7 ½
1 Margareta Roude eine Wittib		1	—	7 ½
1 Christoff Wolfsgruber	25 Jahr	1	—	7 ½
1 Dessen Schwester Ursula Wolfsgruber	18	1	—	7 ½
1 Margareta Keißer	25	1	—	7 ½
39 P Transport		28 ½	64 ½	149 1/4

Personnen	pTransport	Frachten	Zahlt	restirt
39 p Transport		28 ½	64 ½	149 1/4

		Frachten	Zahlt	restirt
8 Christian Hilt von Enderode Ackerman		8	19 ½	40 ½
seine Frau A. M. Catharina				
Sohn Philip Hilt	alt 30 Jahr			
ditto Peter Hilt	alt 21 "			
Tochter Anna Catharina	alt 20 "			
dito Maria Christina	alt 18 "			
dito Maria Elisabet	alt 14 "			
Die Mutter von Christian Hilt				
7 Peter Hilt ein Wittwer von Enderode Ackerman		4	13	17
Tochter Maria Catherina	alt 18 Jahr			
Sohn Johannes	alt 17			
Tochter Aña Margaret	alt 13			
ditto Sophia	alt 7			
Sohn Johannes Justus	alt 4			
Tochter Maria Catherina	alt 2			
NB: von dießen ist ein Kindt gestorben				
5 Henrich Hilt von Enderode Ackerman		3	6 ½	16
seine Frau Anna Maria				
Sohn Johannes	alt 6 jahr			
dito Peter	alt 3			
dito Henrich	alt 2			
6 Fredrich Winchenbach von Enderode Schneider		4	11 ½	18 ½
seine Frau Maria Catharina				
Sohn Jacob Henrich	alt 10 jahr			
Tochter Anna Eva	alt 5			
dito Maria Elisabet	alt 2			
Die Schwieger Mutter Margaret Köhler	alt 63			
5 Johann Köhler von Enderode Ackermann		2 ½	16 ½	1
seine Frau Anna Eva				
Sohn Willem Ernst	6 jahr			
Tochter Anna Maria	4			
Sohn Christian	2			
Die Fracht	_ 7. Pistohl			
6 Jost Ludwig Zimmermann		4 ½	—	33 3/4
seine Frau Anna Gertrut				
Sohn Joh. Jacob	alt 18 Jahr			
Tochter Catherina Elisabet	alt 15			
ditto Anna Margaret	alt 10			
Sohn Johann Jost	alt 3			
8 Peter Liebenzöller von alten Dietz Schneider		6 ½	6	42 3/4
seine Frau Anna Apollina				
Sohn Johan Adam	alt 23 jahr			
Tochter Catharina	alt 21			
Sohn Georg Willem	alt 14			
Tochter Anna Maria	alt 12			
Sohn Christoph	alt 9			
Tochter Anna Margaretha	alt 7			

84	p Transport	61	137 ½	318 3/4

Personnen p Transport		Frachten	Zahlt	restirt
84		61	137 ½	318 3/4

		Frachten	Zahlt	restirt
7 Johann Georg Minck von alten Dietz Buch binder		4	—	30
seine Frau Gerdraut				
Sohn Johann Philip	alt 3 Jahr			
ditto Johannes	alt 2			
Shwieger Mutter Maria Ficklerin	alt 50			
Schwiegerin Maria Ficklerin	alt 30			
Tochterlein Gerdruat	alt 1/4			
3 John Georg Roth von Flohe Stadt Ackermann		2 ½	10	8 3/4
seine Frau Anna Elisabet				
Sohn Johann Conrad	alt 12 jahr			
7 Johann Caspar Claus von Flohe Stadt Ackermann		3 ½	—	26 1/4
seine Frau Agnes				
Sohn Conrad	alt 10 jahr			
Tochter Maria Albertina	alt 8			
Sohn Johannes	alt 6			
ditto Joh. Conrad	alt 4			
ditto Georg Philip	alt 1			
1 Johann Christoffell Roth von ditto Ackermann	alt 29 jahr	1	—	7 ½
1 Joh Georg Hubener von ditto zimmermann		1	—	7 ½
4 Joh. Wilhelm Wagern von E[?]rsbach		2 ½	—	18 3/4
seine Frau Christina Elisabeth				
Tochter Margareta Elisabeth	alt 6 jahr			
Sohn Wilhelm Anton	alt 2			
2 Johann Peter Daurenheim von Flohe Stadt Maurer alt 20 jahr		2	—	15
Schwester Susanna Maria Daurenheim				
1 Johann Jacob Schofener von Langscheid Ackermann 23 jahr		1	—	7 ½
2 Nicolaus Engel von Wolfstein		2	—	15
seine Frau Margaretha				
3 Andreas Doring von ditto		2	—	15
seine Frau Margaretha				
Tochter Catharina Barbara	alt 2 jahr			
7 Johann Nicholaus Schuhmann von Bergen		6	—	45
seine Frau Anna Catherina				
Sohn Johann Bernardt	alt 23 jahr			
ditto Philip Jacob	alt 11			
Tochter Maria Eleonora	alt 21			
ditto Maria Louisa	alt 19			
ditto Maria Elisabet Henriette	alt 8			
3 Carl Staub von Buß Weiler im Elßaß		2	—	15
seine Frau Maria Sibilla				
Sohn Anton Dietrich	2 jahr			
6 Christian Klein von Arbon im Biersteinischen		3	—	22 ½
seine Frau Louisa				
Tochter Anna Elsabet	10 jahr			
Sohn Johan Georg	8			
ditto Philip	3			
Tochter Elisabet Margareta				
131 p Tranport		93 ½	141 ½	552 ½

Personnen p Transport		Frachten	Zahlt	restirt
131 p Transport		93 ½	141 ½	552 ½

		Frachten	Zahlt	restirt
8 Johann Peter Gortz von Neustadt		3 ½	—	26 1/4
seine Frau Anna Maria				
Tochter Anna Clara	12 jahr			
Sohn Johann Carl	10			
Tochter Anna Elisabet	8			
ditto Maria Catharina	3			
shon Christian				
ditto Johann Christian} [i.e. twins] 3 Wochen [weeks old]				
5 Johann Henrich Lang Schul Meister		2 ½	13 ½	12 3/4
seine Frau Anna Catharina				
Sohn Henrich Casper	alt 10 jahr			
Tochter Catharina	alt 2			
ditto Christian	alt 1			
5 Johann Peter Muller von ditto Wagner		3 ½	8 ¼	10 ½
seine Frau Anna Chatharine				
Sohn Jost Henrich	alt 12 jahr			
ditto Wilhelm	alt 1			
Schwieger Mutter Anna Catharina Langin	alt 50			
8 Johann Jost [Mart]ten von Harbach Wagner		6	—	45
sein Frau Anna Maria				
Tochter Anna Christina	alt 21 jahr			
ditto Anna Elisabeth	alt 18			
Sohn Johannes	alt 16			
Tochter Anna Catharina	alt 7			
ditto Anna Cunigunda	alt 5			
ditto Anna Maria	alt 1 ½			
5 Johann Jacob Hein von Schonbach Wollkammer		2 ½	10	8 3/4
seine Frau Anna Margareta				
Sohn Johannes	alt 5 jahr			
Tochter Elisabet	alt 1			
ditto Gertaud	alt 3 Wochen			
4 Heinrich Georg von Gundersheim Ackermann		3	—	22 ½
sen Frau Anna Catharina				
Tochter Margaretha	alt 14 jahr			
Sohn Johann Peter	alt 11			
5 Anton Burckhardt von Fleischbach Kiefer		3	—	22 ½
seine Frau Anna				
Sohn Johann Henrich	alt 9 jahr			
ditto Johannes	alt 4			
Tochter Anna Catharina	alt 3/4			
4 Johann Jost Bornheimer von Sinn Ackermann		3	10	12 ½
siene Frau Anna Dorothea				
Shon Joh. Conrad	alt 13 jahr			
Tochter Anna Dorothea	alt 9			

175 p Transport		120 1/2	189 1/4	713 1/4

Personnen p Transpot		Frachten	Zahlt	restirt
175 p Transport		120 ½	189 1/4	713 1/4
7 Joachim Bornheimer von Shinn		4	—	30
seine Frau Anna Margareta				
Sohn Johann Philip	alt 14 jahr			
ditto Godtfried	alt 11			
Tochter Anna Maria	alt 7			
ditto Dorothea Elisabet	alt 4			
ditto Maria Margaret	alt 1 ½			
8 Dietrich May von ditto Ackermann		7	12	40 ½
seine Frau Anna Maria				
Sohn Jost Henrich Müller Papiermacher	alt 26 jahr			
ditto Frantz Müller dito	alt 25			
Dieses Fau mit ein klein Kind	alt 21			
Tochter Anna Margareta	alt 23			
ditto Anna Catharina	alt 18			
7 Theirß Weber von ditto Schmidt		5 ½	—	41 1/4
sene Frau Anna Catharina				
Sohn Johann Jost Schmidt	alt 33 jahr			
Deßen Frau Anna Elisabet	alt 25			
Tochter Anna Elisabet	alt 1 ½			
obiges Sohn Johannes	alt 11			
Tochter Anna Elisabet	alt 20			
4 Johann Jacob Weyl von Fleischbach		2 ½	9	9 3/4
seine Frau Anna Elisabet				
Tocher Anna Elisabet	alt 9 jahr			
Sohn Johann Conrad	alt 3			
4 Jost Heinrich Beuner von Herborn Maurer		3	—	22 ½
seine Frau Maria Margaretha				
Sohn Johann Jost	alt 11 jahr			
Tochter Maria Elisabet	alt 8			
3 Wilhelm Schnaudill		3	—	22 ½
Seine Frau				
Schwester				
2 Johann Georg Burckhardt von Eichfelden		2	—	15
seine Frau Maria Margaretha				
6 Zacharias Neubert von alten Shönbach		3 ½	—	26 1/4
seine Frau Anna Dorothea				
Tochter Apolena	alt 12 jahr			
Sohn Johann Christoff	alt 10			
ditto Johannes	alt 7			
Tochter Anna Catharina	alt 3 ½			
4 Johan Peter Kram von Eichfelden		2	—	15
seine Frau Elisabet				
Tochter Anna Barbara	2 ½ jahr			
ditto Elisabet	1 1/4			
2 Andreas Elflein von ditto		2	—	15
seine Frau Vernoica [sic - i.e. Veronica]				
222 p Transport		155	201 ¼	951

Personnen	p Transport	Frachten	Zahlt	restirt
222	p Transport	155	201 1/4	951

		Frachten	Zahlt	restirt
4 Nicolaus Bubelreder von Wüstenfeldt seine Frau Elisabet Tochter Catharina Barbara — alt 18 jahr ditto Anna Catharina — alt 10 jahr		3 ½	—	26 1/4
7 Georg Hahn von Aspach seine Frau Anna Margareta Sohn Christoff — alt 17 jahr ditto Hanß Georg — alt 11 ditto Friedrich — alt 10 ditto Georg Friedrich — alt 6 ditto Hanß Philip — alt 2		4 ½	—	33 3/4
6 Georg Appelt von Wüstenfeldt seine Frau Elisabet Sohn Georg Michel — alt 6 jahr ditto Friedrich Carl — alt 3 ½ Tochter Maria Margareta — alt 2 ½ ditto Anna Maria — alt 1/4		2 ½	—	18 3/4
3 Johann Michel Kleinschmidt von Birenstadt seine Frau Anna Maria Sohn Johann Georg Groß — alt 8 jahr		2 ½	—	18 3/4
1 Johann Nicolaus Urff von Aspach		1	—	7 ½
1 Michel Brodtmann von Knitlingen		1	—	7 ½
4 Johann Heinrich Renninger von Eichfelden seine Frau Anna Barbara Tochter Sibilla Barbara — alt 5 jahr Sohn Joh. Martin — alt 1 ½		2 ½	—	18 3/4
3 Johann Matthias Seidensperger von Erlangen seine Frau Maria Susanna Johanna Sohn Johann Jacob — alt 3 Wochen		2	—	15
1 Herr Wilhelm Friedrich Hobbhan von Kitzingen		1	7	—
2 Ein Neulander von Pensilvanien seine Frau		2	—	15
		177 ½	217 1/4	1112 1/4

Louis d'or

4 Herr Secretarius Knöchell
Seine Frau liebste [i.e. dearest wife]
Ein Knecht Nahmens Schmaus [a servant named Schmaus]
Ein Magdt

APPENDIX III

EXCERPTS FROM THE UNITED STATES CENSUS

1790 - 1910

(Data shows location and families with head of households; after 1840 all family members are listed by given name)

Note: *No data is available for the New England States in the 1890 Census as the original records were destroyed by fire.*

FIRST UNITED STATES CENSUS 1790

TOWN	HEAD OF HOUSEHOLD	RESIDENTS
Nobleboro, Mass.	Adam Levenzaler	2 Males age 0-16 3 Males age 16+ 2 Females age 16+
Camdentown, Mass.	Jacob Leavensellers	1 Male age 16+

SECOND UNITED STATES CENSUS - 1800

TOWN   HEAD OF HOUSEHOLD   RESIDENTS

TOWN	HEAD OF HOUSEHOLD	RESIDENTS
Ducktrap, Mass. Page 292	Jacob Lavensaler	1 Male age 10-16 1 Male age 26-45 2 Females age 0-9 1 Female age 16-26
Ducktrap, Mass. Page 297	Stephen Lavensaler	3 Males age 0-9 1 Male age 16-26 1 Female age 0-9 1 Female age 26-45
Canaan, Mass. Page 553	Jacob Levenceller	1 Male age 0-9 1 Male age 26-45 2 Females age 0-9 1 Female age 26-45
Canaan, Mass. Page 539	Stephen Levenceller	2 Males age 0-9 1 Male age 16-26 1 Female age 16-26
Thomaston, Mass. Page 574	Adam Levenseller	2 Males age 0-9 1 Male age 26-45 1 Female age 26-45
Waldoboro, Mass. Page 579	George Levenseller	1 Male age 26-45 1 Female age 0-9 1 Female age 16-26
Waldoboro, Mass. Page 578	Godfrey Levensiller	1 Male age 26-45 3 Females age 0-9 1 Female age 16-26
Waldoboro, Mass. Page 587	John Levenseller	1 Male age 16-26 1 Female age 16-26

THIRD UNITED STATES CENSUS 1810

TOWN	HEAD OF HOUSEHOLD	RESIDENTS
Waldoboro, Mass. Page 088	Gofrred Levenseller	2 Males age 0-9 1 Male age 26-45 1 Female age 0-9 2 Females age 10-16 1 Female age 16-26 1 Female age 26-45
Waldoboro, Mass. Page 088	George Levenseller	3 Males age 0-9 1 Male age 26-45 1 Female age 0-9 1 Female age 10-16 1 Female age 26-45
Waldoboro, Mass. Page ?	John Levenseller	3 Males age 0-9 1 Male age 26-45 1 Female age 0-9 1 Female age 16-26 1 Female age 26-45
Waldoboro, Mass. Page 088	Peter Levenseller	2 Males age 0-9 1 Male age 26-45 2 Females age 0-9 1 Female age 16-26
Thomaston, Mass. Page 100	Adam Levenseller	2 Males age 0-9 2 Males age 10-16 1 Male age 26-45 3 Females age 0-9 1 Female age 10-16 1 Female age 26-45

FOURTH UNITED STATES CENSUS 1820

TOWN	HEAD OF HOUSEHOLD	RESIDENTS
Waldoboro, Maine Page 364	Godfrey Levenseller	1 Male age 0-10 1 Male age 16-26 1 Male age 45+ 1 Female age 16-26 1 Female age 45+
Waldoboro, Maine Page 366	George Levenseller	1 Male age 0-10 1 Male age 10-16 1 Male age 16-18 1 Male age 45+ 3 Females age 0-10 1 Female age 16-26 1 Female age 26-45
Waldoboro, Maine Page 368	John Levenseller	4 Males age 0-10 1 Male age 10-16 1 Male age 16-18 2 Males age 16-26 1 Male age 45+ 1 Female age 10-16 1 Female age 26-45
Waldoboro, Maine Page 366	Peter Levemeller	2 Males age 0-10 1 Male age 10-16 1 Male age 26-45 2 Females age 0-10 1 Female age 10-16 1 Female age 16-26 1 Female age 26-45
Thomaston, Maine Page 257	Adam Levenseller	1 Male age 0-10 1 Male age 16-18 5 Male age 16-26 1 Male age 45+ 1 Female age 0-10 2 Female age 10-16 1 Female age 16-26 1 Female age 45+

FIFTH UNITED STATES CENSUS 1830

TOWN	HEAD OF HOUSEHOLD	RESIDENTS
Waldoboro, Maine Page 119	Godfrey Lavingeller	1 Male age 0-5 1 Male age 15-20 1 Male age 20-30 1 Male age 30-40 1 Male age 50-60 1 Female age 0-5 1 Female age 50-60
Waldoboro, Maine Page 121	George Lavonzeller	1 Male age 5-10 1 Male age 15-20 1 Male age 50-60 2 Female age 10-15 1 Female age 15-20 1 Female age 30-40 1 Female age 50-60
Waldoboro, Maine Page 124	John Lavenzeller	2 Males age 5-10 1 Male age 10-15 2 Males age 15-20 3 Males age 20-30 1 Male age 50-60 1 Female age 10-15 1 Female age 15-20 1 Female age 20-30 1 Female age 40-50
Waldoboro, Maine Page 124	Peter Levonzeller	1 Male age 5-10 1 Male age 15-20 1 Male age 20-30 1 Male age 50-60 1 Female age 5-10 1 Female age 10-15 1 Female age 15-20 1 Female age 40-50
Thomaston, Maine Page 177	Adam Levensellar	1 Male age 10-15 1 Male age 50-60 1 Female age 20-30 1 Female age 30-40 1 Female age 60-70

Fifth U. S. Census
Page 2

TOWN   HEAD OF HOUSEHOLD   RESIDENTS

Thomaston, Maine   Barden Lavendler   1 Male age 0-5
Page 175   1 Male age 30-40
                                           2 Female age 20-30

Brewster, Maine   Lawrence Levenseller   1 Male age 0-5
Page 332   2 Males age 20-30
                                         1 Female age 0-5
                                       1 Female age 15-20
                                       1 Female age 20-30

Lincolnville, Maine   Hezekiah Learsaler   1 Male age 0-5
Page 340   1 Male age 5-10
                                         1 Male age 20-30
                                       1 Female age 0-5
                                       1 Female age 20-30

SIXTH UNITED STATES CENSUS 1840

TOWN   HEAD OF HOUSEHOLD RESIDENTS

TOWN	HEAD OF HOUSEHOLD	RESIDENTS
Waldoboro, Maine	Aaron Levansaler	2 Males age 0-5 1 Male age 30-40 1 Female age 15-20 1 Female age 30-40 1 Female age 60-70
Waldoboro, Maine	George Levanseler	1 Male age 20-30 1 Male age 60-70 1 Female age 20-30 1 Female age 60-70
Waldoboro, Maine	Godfrey Levanseler	1 Male age 70-80 1 Female age 30-40 1 Female age 60-70
Waldoboro, Maine	Jacob Levanseler	1 Male age 30-40 1 Female age 0-5 1 Female age 30-40
Waldoboro, Maine	John Levanseler	1 Male age 10-15 3 Males age 20-30 1 Male age 60-70 1 Female age 15-20 1 Female age 20-30 1 Female age 50-60
Waldoboro, Maine	Moses Levanseler	1 Male age 0-5 1 Male age 30-40 1 Female age 0-5 1 Female age 5-10 1 Female age 20-30
Waldoboro, Maine	Peter Levanseler	1 Male age 15-20 1 Male age 60-70 1 Female age 15-20 1 Female age 60-70
Thomaston, Maine	Joel S. Levensaler	2 Males age 0-5 1 Male age 30-40 1 Female age 20-30

TOWN   HEAD OF HOUSEHOLD RESIDENTS

TOWN	HEAD OF HOUSEHOLD	RESIDENTS
Thomaston, Maine	Lincoln Lavensaler	1 Male age 0-5 1 Male age 20-30 3 Males age 30-40 1 Female age 0-5 1 Female age 15-20 1 Female age 20-30
Thomaston, Maine	Atwood Levensaler	2 Males age 0-5 1 Male age 5-10 1 Male age 40-50 1 Female age 0-5 1 Female age 5-10 1 Female age 20-30 1 Female age 30-40
Thomaston, Maine	Barton Levensaler	1 Male age 0-5 1 Male age 5-10 1 Male age 10-15 1 Male age 40-50 1 Female age 5-10 1 Female age 30-40
Thomaston, Maine	Caleb Levensaler	1 Male age 0-5 1 Male age 30-40 2 Females age 5-10 2 Female age 30-40
Thomaston, Maine	Adam Levensaler	1 Male age 20-30 1 Male age 60-70 1 Female age 20-30 1 Female age 60-70
Washington, Maine	John Leavensaler	1 Male age 0-5 1 Male age 5-10 1 Male age 30-40 1 Female age 30-40
Waldo, Maine	John K. Levensellar	1 Male age 30-40

Sixth U. S. Census
Page 3

TOWN	HEAD OF HOUSEHOLD	RESIDENTS
Waldo, Maine	Leonard M. Levenseller	1 Male age 30-40 1 Female age 5-10 1 Female age 30-40
Lincolnville, Maine	Hezekiah Levensller	2 Males age 0-5 1 Male age 30-40 2 Females age 5-10 1 Female age 30-40
Atkinson, Maine	Jacob Levensellar	1 Male age 0-5 3 Males age 5-10 1 Male age 40-50 2 Females age 0-5 2 Females age 5-10 1 Female age 30-40
Bowerbank, Maine	Peter Levenuller	2 Males age 0-5 2 Males age 5-10 1 Male age 10-15 1 Male age 40-50 1 Female age 30-40
Brewer, Maine	George Levenseller	1 Male age 0-5 2 Males age 5-10 1 Male age 30-40 1 Female age 0-5 1 Female age 10-15 1 Female age 30-40
Brewer, Maine	Lawrence Levenseller	1 Male age 5-10 1 Male age 10-15 1 Male age 20-30 1 Male age 30-40 1 Female age 0-5 1 Female age 5-10 1 Female age 30-40

SEVENTH UNITED STATES CENSUS - 1850

TOWN	NAME	AGE	OCCUPATION	PROPERTY VALUE
Waldoboro	Godfrey Levenseler	80	Farmer	$200
	Christiaina	78	Wife	
Waldoboro	Peter Levenseller	72	Farmer	$900
	Elizabeth	69	Wife	
	Susan W.	15		
Waldoboro	Lawrence Levenseler	49	Farmer	$900
	Rhoda C.	50	Wife	
	Ludlow	18		
	Mary A.	15		
	Margaret	75	Mother	
Waldoboro	Moses Levenseler	46	Farmer	$1,500
	Sally	38	Wife	
	Catherine	15		
	Maria	13		
	Warren	12		
	William	10		
	Mary	8		
	Edward	5		
	Washington	3		
Waldoboro	Jacob Levensaler	42	Carpenter	$200
	Caroline	42	Wife	
	Harriet A.	13		
	Mary A.	8		
	Elijah	6		
Waldoboro	Hector B. Levenseler	30	Joiner	$800
	Louisa	20	Wife	
	Hudson	1		
Waldoboro	Henry Levenseler	30	Carpenter	
	Betsey	27	Wife	
Waldoboro	Cyrus Levenseler	29	Carpenter	$1,000
	Margaret	21	Wife	

Seventh U.S. Census
  Page 2

TOWN	NAME	AGE	OCCUPATION	PROPERTY VALUE
Waldoboro	Aaron Levenseler	49	Shoemaker	$1,000
	Mary	49	Wife	
	Webb	12		
	Aaron	10		
	Maria	8		
	Washington	6		
	Jane Benner	87	(Mother-in-Law)	
Waldoboro	John A. Levenseler	38	Mariner	
	Elcy A.	38	Wife	
	Alonzo	10		
	Oris	6		
	Azro	4		
	Susan Benner	24	(Sister-in-Law)	
Waldoboro	Charles Levenseler	22	Blacksmith	
	Esther M.	21	Wife	
Thomaston	Joel Lavenseler	39	Stonecutter	
	Susan L.	33	Wife	
	Dodge	14		
	Mary E.	9		
Thomaston	Atwood Lavensellaer	44	Merchant	
	Nancy	41	Wife	
	Henry T.	17		
	John	15		
	Augusta	13		
	Adam	11		
	Atwood	9		
	Orris	7		
	Nancy	4		
	Lucuis	7 Mos.		
Thomaston	Caleb Levensaller	45	Merchant	
	Harriet	42	Wife	
	Eley	17		
	Olive	15		
	Joseph	13		
	Harriet	6		
	Raymond	1		

Seventh U.S. Census
  Page 3

TOWN	NAME	AGE	OCCUPATION	PROPERTY VALUE
Thomaston	Mary Lavenseller	76	Adams' Widow	
	Eley	40		
Washington	John Levendaler	38	Farmer	
	Dorothy	38	Wife	
	Thomas	16		
	James	14		
	Mary J.	12		
	Susan	10		
	Lucy	8		
	Warren	5		
	Sarah	3		
	Emily	1		
Bowerbank	Peter Levensaler	56	Farmer	
	Betsy	45	Wife	
	Joseph	23		
	Sally	19		
	J.	16		
	John	14		
	Debrah	9		
Sebec	Thomas Lavenseller	26	Farmer	
	Vesta	22	Wife	
	James	1		
Atkinson	Jacob Levensaler	54	Farmer	
	Matha	50	Wife	
	Joan	22		
	J.	20		
	Betsy	15		
	Martha	10		
	Elinor	15		
	John	18		
	Laphin	18		
	Jacob	15		
	Moses	12		
	Leonard	8		
Waldo	Leonard Levansaler	48	Farmer	
	Evaline	41	Wife	
	Rebecca Johnson	19		
	John W.	2		

110

Seventh U. S. Census
  Page 4

TOWN	NAME	AGE	OCCUPATION	PROPERTY VALUE
Waldo	John K. Levanseller	43	Farmer	
	Sarah W.	26	Wife	
	R. Ellen Gay	14		
	Gilbert	9 Mos.		
Camden	Morapat Levanseller	78		
Boston Ward 10	Jenna A. Levenseller	29	Piano Maker	
Suffolk	------- Levensellar	29	Piano Forte Maker	
Boston Ward 11	Austin Levanselear	27	Piano Forte Maker	
Suffolk	Mary E.	25	Wife	
	Frank E.	4 Mos.		
	Francis A. Paul	23		

EIGHTH UNITED STATES CENSUS - 1860

TOWN	NAME	AGE	OCCUPATION	PROPERTY VALUE
Waldoboro	Peter Levanseller	82	Tailor	
	Elizabeth	80	Wife	
Waldoboro	Loring Levanseller	60	Farmer	$1,500
	Rhoda	60	Wife	
	John McAndrew	24	Laborer	
	Rebecca Oliver	70	Domestic	
Waldoboro	Moses Levanseller	56	Farmer	$2,000
	Sally	48	Wife	
	William	19	Laborer	
	Mary A.	17		
	Edward F.	14		
	Moses W.	12		
Waldoboro	Jacob Levanseller	52	Farmer	
	Caroline	50	Wife	
	Elizah S.	16	Farm Laborer	
	Jane Ann	88	Mother	
Waldoboro	John A. Levanseller	48	Merchant	$1,000
	Elcy	42	Wife	
	Alonzo	19	Sailor	
	Oris	16	Clerk	
	Azro	14		
	Susan	10		
	Florance	2		
Waldoboro	Cyrus Levenseller	45	School Teacher	$800
	Margret	31	Wife	
	Lewis K.	1		
Waldoboro	Hector Levenseller	43	House Joiner	$700
	Louisa	30	Wife	
	Hudson	11		
	Hattie	9		
Waldoboro	Henry Levenseller	40	Ship Carpenter	$150
	Betsy	35	Wife	
	Alexis	10		
	Laura A.	7		
	Mary A. Kaler	23	Milliner	

TOWN	NAME	AGE	OCCUPATION	PROPERTY VALUE
Waldoboro	Ludlow Levanseller	28	Blacksmith	
	Leonora	24	Wife	
	Willford S.	3		
Waldoboro	Mathias Welt	60	Farm Laborer	
	Austin Levenseller	14		
Waldoboro	Christianna Benner	67		
	Aaron Levanseller	59	Shoemaker	
Waldoboro	Lincoln Lavanseller	16	Farm Laborer	
Thomaston	Lincoln Levensaler	58	Farmer	
	George E.	23	Clerk	
	Charles L.	17	Mariner	
	Caleb	11		
	John W.	9		
Thomaston	William Levensaler	30	Mariner	
	Ann S.	28	Wife	
	Florence W.	3mos.		
Thomaston	Ann J. Levensaler	58	Barden (Widow)	$2,600
	Edward R.	27	Painter	
	Thomas H.	26	Mariner	
Thomaston	Atwood Levansaler	60	Merchant	$3,600
	Nancy	52	Wife	
	Mary L.	27		
	John C.	25	Cashier	
	Augusta K.	23		
	Atwood	19	Teacher	
	Orris	17	Clerk	
	Nancy G.	13		
Thomaston	Alexis Levansaler	49		$1,000
	(Living on the Farnsworth Farm)			
Thomaston	Dodge Levansaler	24	Mason	$600
	Bertha	21	Wife	
	Caroline F.	9 mos.		
	Mary E.	18		$200

Eighth U.S. Census
Page 3

TOWN	NAME	AGE	OCCUPATION	PROPERTY VALUE
Thomaston	Caleb Levinsaler	55	Master Mariner	$15,000
	Harriett	52	Wife	
	Joseph	23	Mariner	
	Harriett	16		
	Raymond	10		
Camden	Washington Levensaler 16 (Living on the Ida Casner Farm)			
Camden	Anesisto Levensaler 18 (Living in the James Pottle Household as a Servant)			
Camden	Mary Levensiller 59 (Living with Daughter Mary Daily)			
Washington	John Levenseller	49	Farmer	$1,460
	Dorothy	48	Wife	
	Lucy	18		
	Warren	15		
	Sarah	13		
	Peter	12		
	Emily	11		
	Alice	10		
	Abba	9		
Atkinson	Stephen Levensailor	27	Farmer	
Atkinson	Betsy Levensailor	25		
Atkinson	Jacob Levensailor	62	Farmer	
	Martha	60	Wife	
	Jacob	24	Farm Laborer	
	Moses	22		
	Martha	20		
	Leonard	18		
	Mary E.	15		
	Rose E.	5		
Washington	Thomas Levenseller	26	Farmer	$1,065
	Mary	24	Wife	
	Caroline	1		

TOWN	NAME	AGE	OCCUPATION	PROPERTY VALUE
Bowerbank	Peter Levensailor	62	Farmer	
	Betsy	52	Wife	
	Silas	28	Laborer	
	Peter	26	Farmer	
	John	22	Farm Laborer	
Bowerbank	Joseph Levensalor	32	Shingle Maker	
	Francis D.	24	Wife	
	Harrietta	6 mos.		
Sebec	Thomas Levensaler	36	Lumber Laborer	
	Vesta	33	Wife	
	Vinson	11		
	Deborah Ann	4		
	Frank	2		
	Cynthia Douglap	14		
Sebec	Sally Levensalor	56		
	Stephen	34	Merchant	
	Sheba	28		
	Laura	6		
	Stephen J.	2		
Lincolnville	Samuel Levensaler	23	Ship Carpenter	
Lincolnville	Hezekiah Levensalor	59	Farmer	
	Margret	61	Wife	
	Margret A.	25		
	Francis H.	23	School Teacher	
	Samuel A.	21	Ship Carpenter	
	Francis E.	5		
Waldo	Leonard Levenseller	60	Farmer	
	Eveline	58	Wife	
	Wesley	14		
	Rodney	11		
Waldo	John K. Levensailor	52	Farmer	
	Sarah	36	Wife	
	Gilbert	10		
	Charles	5		
	John M.	1 mon.		

NINTH UNITED STATES CENSUS - 1870

TOWN	NAME	AGE	OCCUPATION	PROPERTY VALUE
Waldoboro	Alexis Levanseller	20	Mariner	
	Laura	17	Wife	
Waldoboro	Jacob Levanmuller	62	Farmer	
	Caroline S.	62	Wife	
Waldoboro	Hector Levanseller	52	Carpenter	
	Louisa	41	Wife	
	Hattie	19		
Waldoboro	Loring Levenseller	70	Farm Laborer	
	Rhoda	70	Wife	
Waldoboro	Aaron Levanseller	69	Bootmaker	
	Mary	69	Wife	
Waldoboro	Moses Levanseller	66	Farmer	$2,000
	Sallie	58	Wife	
	Edward F.	24		
	Moses W.	22		
Waldoboro	John A. Levanseller	57	Truckman	$1,100
	Elcy	54	Wife	
	Orris	27	Stonecutter	
	Susan A.	20	Domestic	
	Florance	12		
Waldoboro	Cyrus Levanseller	55	Fisherman`	$800
	Margret	41	Wife	
	Lewis K.	10		
	Ada B.	6		
Waldoboro	Elizabeth Levanseller	45	Housekeeper	$600
Waldoboro	William Levanseller	29	School Teacher	$1,000
	Lizzie	21	Wife	
Waldoboro	Elijah Levanseller	25	Farm Laborer	
	Martha	23	Wife	

TOWN	NAME	AGE	OCCUPATION	PROPERTY VALUE
Rockport MA.	Alonzo Levenseller	30	Fisherman	
	Mary E.	26	Wife	
Waldoboro	Ludlow Levansellar	38	Blacksmith	$600
	Leonora	34	Wife (Millner)	
	Wilfred	12		
Rockport MA.	Azro Levenseller	23	Fisherman	
	Mary E.	19	Wife	
	Mary E.		7mos. (Born October 1870)	
Thomaston	Joseph Levensaler	33	Master Mariner	
	Emma	25	Wife	
	William M.	10 mos.		
Thomaston	John C. Levensaler	35	Judge of Probate	
	Mary L.	24	Wife	
	Lizzie S.	1		
Thomaston	Adam Levensales	31	Grocer	
	Agusta H.	33	Wife	
	Nancy	21	Sister	
Thomaston	Caleb Levensaler	65	Master Mariner (Retired)	
	Harriet	62	Wife	
Thomaston	Raymond Levensaler	20	Grocery Clerk	
	Henretta	18	Wife	
Thomaston	Atwood Levensaler	28	Lime Burner	
	Harriet	26	Wife	
Thomaston	Ann Levensaler	69	Widow of Bardon	
	Thomas H.	33	Mariner	
Lincolnville	Carrie Levensalor	17	Boarder with Andrew McCobb	
Lincolnville	Heziacha Levensalor	69	Farmer	
	Margaret	72	Wife	
	Frank E.	15		
	Hebert Robbins	11	Servant	

Ninth U. S. Census
Page 3

TOWN	NAME	AGE	OCCUPATION	PROPERTY VALUE
Searsmont	Frank Levenseler	28	Millman	
	Jane H.	27	Wife	
	John W.	3 mos.		
Atkinson	Moses Levensalor	32	Farmer	
	Roxy	24	Wife	
	Alice C.	7		
	Hattie	3		
	Lucy	3		
	Merritt	9 mos.		
	Martha	70	Mother	
Bowerbank	Siles Levensailor	37	Farmer	
	Peter	85	Grandfather	
	John	30	Brother	
	Peter	78	Father	
	Betsy	66	Mother	
	Fred	7		
	John	6		
	Mabel	3		
	Harry	2		
Bowerbank	Sally Levensailor	65	Widow of Joseph	
Sebec	Thomas Levensalor	47	Shingle Mill Hand	
	Vesta	44	Wife	
	Deborah	14		
	Frank	12		
	Lizzie	9		
	Thomas	7		
	Effie	4		

TENTH UNITED STATES CENSUS - 1880

TOWN	NAME	AGE	OCCUPATION	COMM.
Waldoboro	William Levenseller	39	Grocer	
	Liza	31	Wife	
	Fred A.	9		
	Amos	1		
	Moses W.	32	Grocer	(Brother)
Waldoboro	Murray F. Benner	37		
	Susan A.	29	Wife	
	Elsa Levensaler	63	Mother-in-Law	
Waldoboro	Hector Levenseller	63	House Carpenter	
	Thomas Fitzpatrick	28	Son-in-Law	
	Hattie	29		
	Nettie	3	Grand Daughter	
Waldoboro	Margret Levensiller	51	Housekeeper	
	Lewis K.	20		
Waldoboro	Alonzo Levenseller	39	Fisherman	
	Mary E.	37	Wife	
	Lizzie F.	10		
	John A.	5		
Waldoboro	Moses Levenseller	76	Farmer	
	Sally	68	Wife	
	Edward	34	Farmer	
Waldoboro	Rhoda Levenseller	82		(Living with Daughter Mary A. Shuman)
Waldoboro	Jacob Levenseller	73	Farmer	
Waldoboro	Cyrus Levenseller	65		
Waldoboro	Elijah Levenseller	36	Ship Carpenter	
	Martha E.	33	Wife	
	Olive Lash	64	Mother-in-Law	
Washington	Aldana Levenseller	27	Servant	(Sister-in-Law to Everett Cunningham)
Washington	John Levenseller	69	Farmer	(Sick with Fever)
	Dorothy	69	Wife	

Tenth U. S. Census
Page 2

TOWN	NAME	AGE	OCCUPATION	COMM.
Washington	Thomas Levenseller	45	Farmer	
	Mary	44	Wife	
	Louise	17	Teacher	
	Pearlie	10		
	Flora	4		
Thomaston	Caleb Levenseler	75	Shipmaster	(Retired)
	Kate	73	Wife	
	Harriet	36		
Thomaston	William Levensaler	51	Sailor	
Thomaston	Henry Levensaler	49	Physician	
	Mary S.	30	Wife	
	Nettie M.	5		
	Edwin S.	3		
Thomaston	John C. Levensaler	45	Bank Cashier	
	Mary L.	34	Wife	
	Lizzie A.	11		
Thomaston	Adam Levensaler	41	Grocer	
Thomaston	Atwood Levensaler	39	Merchant	
	Henrietta	28	Wife	
	Jane A.	9		
	Eliza K.	7		
	Alfred W.	4		
Lincolnville	Francis Levanseller	43	Farmer	
	Cynthia	29	Wife	
	Addie	6		
	Edgar	4		
	Janie M.	3		
	Mary	81	Mother	
	Luci Susie	31	Sister-in-Law	
Waldo	Sarah Levenseler	56	Housekeeper (John K. Widow)	
	Gilbert	30	Farmer	
	Charles	24	Farmer	
	John	20		

TOWN	NAME	AGE	OCCUPATION	COMM.
Holden	George V. Levensaler	74	Farmer	
	Nancy	70	Wife	
Holden	Hiram Levensaler	36	Farmer	
	Elizabeth	36	Wife	
	Arthur R.	13		
	Maud M.	11		
	Grace D.	10		
	Georgia	7		
	Willie	5		
	Alice E.	28	Teacher	(Sister)
Holden	Audrey Levensaler	46	Farmer	
	Susan	42	Wife	
	Addie	19		
	Percy S.	17		
	Flora	10		
	Nellie	7		
	Harry M.	4		
Atkinson	Moses Leavensalor	41	Farmer	
	Roxie	39	Wife	
	Alice	17		
	Hattie	15		
	Lucy	13		
	Edward M.	10		
	Agnes	8		
	Aurther S.	5		
	Lewis T.	2		
Sebec	Thomas Leivinsailor	56	Farmer	
	Vista	53	Wife	
	Frank	22		
	Lizzie	19		
	Thomas Jr.	18		
	Effie	14		
Searsmont	John W. Levenseller	10		Nephew of John Moore
Searsmont	Frank Levenseller	25	Farmer	
	Mary E.	24	Wife	
	Charles	6		
	Judson	2		

Tenth U. S. Census
Page 4

TOWN	NAME	AGE	OCCUPATION	COMM.
Sebec	Jame Levensailor	31	Woolen Millworker	
	Mary E.	30	Wife	
Bowerbank	Peter Levensailor	42		
	Betsy	72	(Mother)	
Bangor	Leonard Levinseller	32		
25 Pine St.	Eliza	32	Wife	
	Mabel	3		
Garland	Stephen Levensolar	47		
	Flora	50	Wife	
	Ella F.	15		
	Mary A.	12		
	Carrie	9		
	Harry T.	6		
	John W.	3		
	Alfred S.	1		
Belfast	Charles Levenseller	52		
	Esther	51	Wife	
	Nettie	18		
	Pling Jones	37	Son-in-Law	
	Fannie L.	28		
	Adian	4	Grandson	
LaGrange	Ernst Leavensailor	10		Boarder with Wesley Hall
Howard	John Levenseller	41		
	Flora	26	Wife	
	Josia	2		
	Flora	1		
Tauton MA	Warren Levanseller	34		
Linden St.	Mary	34	Wife	
	W. Clinton	7		
Providence RI	Azro Levenseller	34	Painter (5months/Yr.)	
Oxford St.	Mary E.	27	Wife	
	Mary Ellen	10	Student	
	Walter L.	7		
Providence RI	Mary Levensaller	10		Boarder with Fred W. Folsom

TWELFTH UNITED STATES CENSUS - 1900

TOWN	NAME	AGE		BIRTH MONTH/YEAR	
Waldoboro	Edward F. Levensaler	54		7	1845
	Mary L.	36		6	1863
	Florence B.	6		10	1893
	Laura C.	50	Cousin	5	1850
Waldoboro	Moses W. Levensaler	52		6	1847
	Mary E.	54		6	1845
	Ruth E.	15		6	1884
Waldoboro	Lewis K. Levensaler	39		8	1860
	Lenora	26		12	1873
	Velma	3		2	1897
	Marion	1		1	1899
	Ruth	6 mos.		4	1900
Waldoboro	Elijah S. Levensaler	56		1	1844
	Martha	52		11	1847
Waldoboro	Elsie Levensaler Living with William Weeks	84	Mother-in-Law	1	1816
Waldoboro	Orris Levensaler	55		1	1845
	Sarah	40		1	1860
Waldoboro	Walter L. Levensaler	27		1	1873
	Lura B.	24		4	1876
	Aurther E.	1		6	1898
	Raymond E.	7 mos.		10	1899
	Azro	55	Father	5	1845
Waldoboro	William Weeks	45		5	1855
	Florance C.	42		9	1857
	Elsie	84	Mother-in-Law	1	1816
Waldoboro	William H. Levensaler	59		9	1840
	Lizzi	51		9	1848
	Guy	21		11	1878
Friendship	Wilfred Levenseller	41		8	1858
	Julie	38		10	1861
	George	16		3	1884

TOWN	NAME	AGE	BIRTH MONTH/YEAR	
Waldo	Sarah Levanseller	76	4	1824
	Charles A.	44	8	1855
	John L.	40	5	1860
Waldo	Gilbert C. Levanseller	50	8	1849
	Sarah	47	3	1853
	Jennie G.	6	1	1894
	Mary	5	5	1895
Thomaston	John C. Levenseller	65	5	1835
Gleason St.	Mary L.	54	10	1845
	Lizzie S.	31	3	1869
	Walter Jacob	56 Brother-in-Law	2	1844
	Ann Starrett	57 Sister-in-Law	10	1842
	Niomi O'Brien	Daughter-in-Law		
Thomaston	Harriett G. Levensaler	55	4	1845
	Elsie L. Burges	67	9	1832
Thomaston	Augustia H. Levensales	63	1	1837
	Thomas Andrews			
Thomaston	Atwood Levensaler	59	3	1841
	Harriett P.	47	10	1852
	James A.	29	3	1871
	Eliza	27	1	1873
	Alfred W.	24	5	1876
	1 Boarder			
	1 Servant			
Thomaston	Charles Levensaler	27	8	1873
	Lizzie	27	10	1873
	Eva	5	4	1895
	Hilda	4	1	1896
	Harney	3	8	1897
Thomaston	Mary S. Levensaler	50	12	1849
Willimantic	Fred H. Levensaler	36	12	1863
Maine	Mary C.	36	7	1864
	Mary B.	10	12	1889
	Ellen A.	7	9	1892

TOWN	NAME	AGE	BIRTH MONTH/YEAR
Washington	Thomas Levensaler	65	11 1834
	Pearl S.	38	8 1861
	Leola	22 Daug.-In-Law	5 1878
	Herbert	2 Grandson	4 1898
	Florence	23	12 1876
Augusta 88 Grove St.	Margret Levensaler Living with Elmer E. Newbert	70 Mother-In Law	5 1830
Waterville Elmwood Hotel	Walter Levensaler Servant to Henry E. Judkins	20	1880
Winterport	Rodney Levinseller	50	2/02/1850
	Emma C.	46	7/25/1853
	Irving W.	22	7/02/1877
	Hubert R.	14	10/22/1866
Hampden	Leonard Levenseller	52 Born in Canada	4 1848
	Eliza	51	7 1848
	Mabel	23	5 1877
	Thomas McDonough	23 Boarder	12 1876
Belfast	Esther Levensaler	71	5 1829
	Fanny L. Jones	49	8 1850
	Adrian F.	24 Grandson	5 1876
Rockland	Frank Levenseler	43	12 1856
	Mary	43	1 1857
	Judson	22	9 1877
	May Woods	18 Niece	3 1822
Lincolnville	Frank Levenseler	63	10 1836
	Cynthia	49	2 1851
	Fred A. Heal	24	11 1875
Holden	Hiram Levenseller	55	4 1845
	Lizzie	55	4 1845
	Charles C. Huston	46 Boarder	7 1854
	Mary E. Huston	43 Boarder	12 1857
	Renah R. Huston	16 Boarder	2 1884
	Herbert L. Huston	14 Boarder	8 1885

TOWN	NAME	AGE	BIRTH MONTH/YEAR	

| Brunswick | Alfred Levensaler (Bowdin College Senior) | 24 | 5 | 1876 |

| Dexter | Ruby W. Lavenseller (Living with Gustave Weymouth - Grandfather) | 2 | 2 | 1898 |

Dexter	Arthur Lavenseller	33	8	1866
	Bertha E.	31	4	1869
	Earl A.	6	7	1893

Holden	Audrey Levenseller	66	11	1833
	Susan	61	2	1839
	Percy	37	5	1863
	Melvin	23	3	1877
	Grace	26 Daugh-in-Law	4	1879
	Rebecca Kingsbury	81 Boarder	6	1818

Bangor	Frank Leavenseller	42	3	1858
	Blanche	32	9	1867
	Maud	14	7	1885
	Ivy B. 3 Boarders	11	3	1889

Sebec	Vinton J. Levensailor	51	5	1849
	Mary	50	8	1849
	Armina Robinson	72 Mother-in-Law	9	1827
	Winfield S.	18	2	1882
	Noah B. Berce	Boarder		

Sebec	Vesta S. Levensaler	73	3	1827
	Williard	10 Grandson	2	1890
	Eva	8 Granddaughter	5	1892
	Harold	5 Grandson	9	1894

Abbot	Thomas Levensaler	37	7	1862
	Mary E.	24	2	1876
	Clara Buxton	Boarder		

Brownville	Silas Levensaler	66	2	1834
	Drusilla	56	8	1844
	Alice	7 Granddaughter	7	1893

TOWN	NAME	AGE	BIRTH MONTH/YEAR	
Atkinson	Stephen Leavensaler	67	4	1833
	Flora	50	1	1850
	Harry	26	3	1874
	John W.	23	11	1876
	Alfred S.	21	2	1879
	Stephen	18	2	1882
	Mable L.	14	12	1885
	Jennie	8	9	1891
	Ernst	4	6	1895
Atkinson	Merritt E. Leavensailor	30	9	1869
	Nellie E.	25	9	1874
Dover	Alfred Levensellar	21	1	1879
	Anson Robinson	Boarder		
Indian Terr.	Peter Levensaler	59	8	1841
Numer 3	Luther Gerrish	Boarder		
LaGrange	Fred L. Levansella	35	1	1864
	Mary C.	35		1864
	Linnie Ashness	25 Sister	1	1875
	Mary B.	11		1889
	Ellen B.	8		1892
	Eva M.	5 Boarder	6	1894
Monson	John Levensellar	62	1	1838
	Flora E.	46	5	1854
	Josie E.	22	1	1878
	Willie L.	19	6	1881
	Scott E.	15	4	1885
	Clarence	11	4	1889
	Winifred	8	1	1892
Portsmouth	John A. Levenseller	24		
Rhode Island	Private U. S. Army, Assigned out of Fort Hamilton, Brooklyn, N.Y. Company N. 5th Artillery. Born in Glocester, Mass. in 1876.			
Elizabeth N.J.	Elmer Lavanseller	36	2	1864
46 Sayre St.	Mary	29	3	1871
	Edward S.	7 mos.	10	1889

Twelfth U. S. Census
  Page 6

TOWN	NAME	AGE	BIRTH MONTH/YEAR	
Boston 709 Cambridge St.	Esta N. Levensaler	71	5	1829
Everett MA 77 School St.	William Levensaler	36	1	1864
	Lizzie	56	4	1844
	Blanche	20	6	1880
	Boarders in the Harmon Turrell Household			
Bridgewater	Pearl F. Levensaler	30	12	1869
	Laura M.	21	5	1879
	Clifton	4	10	1896
Taunton 56 Lynden St.	Warren Levensaler	54	7	1845
	Mary J.	54		1846

THIRTEENTH UNITED STATES CENSUS -1910

TOWN	NAME	AGE	OCCUPATION	REMARKS
Waldoboro	Orris Levensaler	66	Marbleworker	Owns Shop
48 Jefferson	Sarah (Magune)	50		Born in MA
Waldoboro	Murray F. Benner	67		
50 Jefferson	Susan (Levensaler)	59		
	Chester A.	27	Nephew	
Waldoboro	Fred A. Levinsaler	39	Electrician	
70 Jefferson	Maude M.	35		
	Edith E.	5		
	Margaret A.	3		
Waldoboro	William Levensaler	69	Real Estate Agent	
73 Jefferson	Elizabeth (Waltz)	61		
	Guy A.	31		
Waldoboro	William Weeks	54	Farmer	
186 Orfs	Florance (Levensaler)	52		
Corner Rd.	James A.	5	Grandson	
Waldoboro	Edward Levensaler	64	Farmer	
383 Union	Lizzie (Hahn)	46		
Waldoboro	Lewis K. Levensaler	49	Farm Laborer	
97 Friendship	Lenora (Day)	47		
	Velma	13		
	Marion E.	11		
	Hazel M.	10		
	Harold D.	8		
	Doris R.	6		
	Alton	5		
	Arnold P.	3		
	Appie	1		
Waldoboro	Moses Levensaler	62	Retail Clothier	
1591 Main	Mary E. (Miller)	64		
	Ruth E.	25		
Waldoboro	Azro Levensaler	64	Inside Painter	
201Nobleboro	Emma S. (Campbell)	50		Wife born in Nova Scotia
Waldoboro	Laura Levensaler	55		
9 Main St.				

Thirteenth U. S. Census
Page 2

TOWN	NAME	AGE	OCCUPATION	REMARKS
Atkinson 48 Mills Rd.	Merritt Levenseller Nellie	40 35	Farmer	
Atkinson 51 Mills Rd.	Ernest Levenseller (Boarding With His Uncle Eward Sidelinker)	15	Farm Laborer	
Brownville 281 Vanham	John Levensaller	46	Machinist	
Dover 52 Pleasent	Scot Levensailor	21	Weaver	Boarding
Dover 259 Elm St.	Willie Levensailor Emelie Gordon Kennith	28 25 4 3	Wool Finisher	
Sebec 119	Peter Levensailor	73		Retired
Sebec 125	Thomas Levensailor Mary E. William H. Eva M. Harold T. Vesta E. Leon V.	47 35 20 17 15 7 5	Watch Repairer	
Belfast 123	Esther Levensaler	80	Farmer	
Waldo 78	Gilbert Levenseller Sarah E. Jennie E. Mary E. Charles A.	60 57 16 14 54	Farmer	Brother
Waldo	John Levenseller Julin Margerett J. Margery F.	40 28 3 9 mos.	Saw Mill Employee	

TOWN	NAME	AGE	OCCUPATION	REMARKS
Searmont	Frank Levenseller	73	Farmer	
16	Howard A. Elms			Son-in-Law
Winterport	Emma Levenseller	57		
114	Irving W.	32		
	Walter	28		
Bangor	Frank Levensellar	51	Saw Filer	
17 Ncay St.	Blanche	44		
	Ivy	21		
Everett MA	Maud B. Levansaler	20		Living with
3 Thurman	Averil U.	5 Mos.		Father George
				Underwood
Thomaston	Charles Levenseller	36	Quarryman/Limewasher	
	Lizzie M.	36		
	Eva B.	16		
	Hilda N.	14		
	Harry L.	12		
Thomaston	Mary L. Levenseller	60		
Gleason St.	Lizzie S.	41		
Thomaston	Harry Levensaler	42		(Inmate at the State Prison)
Thomaston	James Levenseller	39		
Knox St.	Ann A.	40		
	Henretta	57		Mother
Washington	Thomas Levensaler	74		
	Amilia	59		
	Floria	34		
Washington	Clifton Levensaler	12		Servant for Alonzo Grotten
San Francisco	Caleb Levensaler	36		
California	Ida	32		
	John D.	5		
	Frances	3		

Thirteenth U. S. Census
Page 4

TOWN	NAME	AGE	OCCUPATION	REMARKS
Napa	Charles Levensaler	65		
California	Lujetta	46		
	Edith	17		
	Olive	12		
	Russell	10		
Lakeport	Burgess Levensaler	32		
California	Julia D.	30		
	James L.	2		
	Joseph G.	73		Father
Everett MA	Walter Levensaler	38	House Carpenter	
239 Main St	Lura B.	32		
	Arthur E.	12		
	Raymond E.	9		
	Leon W.	4		

INTERPRETATION OF THE MAY 30, 1753
PETITION TO GOVERNOR PHIPPS ESQ.
MASSACHUSETTS BAY, AT BOSTON

PROVINCE OF THE   )   To the Honble Spencer Phipps Esq.
)   Lieut: Gov: & Commander in Chief
MASSACHUSETTS BAY)   for the time being of said Provice, The
)   Honble his Majestic Council and
)   House of Representatives in General
)   Court Assembled. May 30, 1753

The Memoriall of Jacob Haterick and other German Protestants.

Humbly therewith,

                That upon the encouragement of this
government in consequence of the grant of land for the settlement of a
township on certain conditions therein mentioned, we were induced at
a very great expense to come over into America and arrived at Boston
in the month of November in the year 1751. That a number of us not
being able to pay so great an expense as our passage form Germany
necessialy involved us in, we have been obliged to go to labour with
our hands in order to discharge said expense, which some of us have
now cleared.

       Our intention being to settle on the tract of land laid out at
Massachusetts tract on the western borders of this province, and in
order to proceed in a regular manner, we now apply to this honrble
court for their further direction and are now ready to atend such
orders as shall seem necessary, justly hoping for al that
encouragement and assistance our present circumstances may stand
in need of and we in duty bound that ever pray.

Signed:

Thirty-One Settlers

ANSWER FROM THE GENERAL COURT
TO THE PETITION OF MAY 30, 1753

Judicial House of Representatives   June 6, 1753

Read and it appearing that in the year 1749. This court granted four townships an order to encourage foreign protestants to come and settle in this government, and grants farm of land in each said townships to Mr. Joseph Crellius in case he caused it to be settled in each of said townships. One hundred and twenty families by the time now in said grants, but it appearing also that the said Mr. Crellius has failed and being toward said settlements, and that the poor petitioners are left without and aid.

Therefore, noted that Col. Cartridge and Col. Worthington with such as the general board shall injoin be a committee to lay out thirth-one house lots not exceeding ten acres each, contiguous to each other in the German township so called at Fort Massachusetts and also so much if the internal land in said township for of said house lots as shall make up ea. 1 2/3 all offered. Considered with relative to quantity and quality what the petitioners are at liberty to settle upon and improve. Said lands agreeable to the full General Court and further that said committee lay out in said township four more house lots, not to exceed ten acres each, one for the first church for the protestant minster, one for the ministry, and one for the school and meeting house the remainder of the intervale land in forth-eight equal house lots with aforesaid relation to quality and quantity of these lots three will be set aside, one for the minister and one for the ministry and one for the school, and that the for said committee admit fourty-five settlers in addition to the petitioners, each of which forty-five settlers shall pay to the said committee for the use of the government the sum of six pounds thirteen schillings and four pence and shall give bond in the sum of fifty pounds to said committee to perform the like conditions of settlement from this time forward as were injoined in the orginal grant of the township, and that in all after divisions of land in said township the petitioners shall each of them have 1 2/3 part thereof and that the remainder of the township shall be divided first among the admitted settlers with the public rights aforementioned each with equal parts and that the original grant made in said township to Mr. Joseph Crellius is hereby declared void and forfeited to the government he not having complyed with the conditions thereof.

Sent up for concurrence

A. And is as much as the petitioners have signified their desires that some English families may be admitted as settlers with them on the same lands that therefore

B. We conceed to the aforesaid by allowable

INTERPRETATION OF THE MAY 1754
PETITION TO WILLIAM SHIRLEY ESQ, GOVERNOR
MASSACHUSETTS BAY, AT BOSTON

Most Noble Born, Most Grace, Most Honoured Lord Gouvernor:

Your excellency will excuse the liberty, we poor deserted Germans take, in wording our most humble petition to you; Considering: that about 130 families containing almost 500 souls, live at Broad Bay, being thus abandoned, that in case there should happen a war, (which is common report) having no garrison, we must be exposed to the danger, of being killed by the Indians one after another, in our own houses. If we should build 2:or 3: Garrisons, meerly any old settlers being provided with provisions for a couple of weeks, by themselves, and the newcomers of the Jar 1753: by Mr. Waldo: but none of those settlers that arrived in the Jar 1752: We most desperate to starve for hunger: over and besides, for want of Powder, Bullets, and flints, we should can not defend ourselves. Therefore, we poor deserted subjects in common, implore your Excellentcy Gracousness (:regauding you as the father of the land:) to assist us, your poor children, for the sake of god, and to deliver us from those miseries.

We never shall dare to prescribe your Excellentcy what to do, or in what manner we shall be saved; Your wisdom will supplicate to you by what means we poor Deserted Germans must be Supported, in the aforementtioned points by your Excellentcy Favors. We are in the utmost Subjection, Your Excellentcy.
Broad Bay the 13 May, 1754:

Most Humble and
Most Obedient Subjects:

Joh: Martin Raiser
Phillip Rimmer
Valonbin Jung
Mathaus Rimmele
Jacob Walt
John Jacob Ulmer
Conrad Troupel
John Heirnith Dumuth
Lausentius + Seitz
Casimir Losth
Paulus Dorthlerman

Johann Ulmer Cap:
Jacob Deis
Joh: Martin Ulmer
Phillip + Vogler
Fran + Eislle
David Rominger
Jacob Laus

PS: Those subscriptions serve, for all the settlers, who living very much dispursed can not alway assemble.
    Jn;

INTERPRETATION OF THE AUGUST 1757
PETITION TO THE
MASSACHUSETTS GENERAL COURT

May it Please Your Houners

    To receive in this few lines, an account of that Griefances, of the most part of the settlers at Broad Bay. The Continuation of the Waare, and the cruelty of the Indian Enemy Used here, has been a terror to us and also a Great hinderance to our labor; Tho we bare all that with patiece, as long we were Capable to maintain in some measure, our large Famelys, but now with Tears in our eyes, must acquaint Your Honors that our harvest is so miserable, as ever been Known by Mankind, so that most of Us, will not be able to reap the Seed, which we sowed with hard Labour, and in danger of our lives, owing to the deep Snow, which lasted till the middle of May and then the Great drought which followed; We see no way to keep us, and Large Famelys from Starving as the respective Towns in the Western parts refuse to receive any of us; we therefore hope Your Honours will be pleased, to take our deplorable case into Consideration, what damage it would accure to the Eastern parts, in case such a Number of Famelys should be forced to breakup, as we are at the borders of the Enemy, certainly the rest of the Settlements, between this and North Yarmouth would be obliged to follow us, as they also would be exposed and incapable to Stand their Ground, and such Number of Famely's would certainly become a Great Charge and Trouble, to this Provins. We therefore Humbly implore Your Honours mercy to Allowe onely an Allowance of Provisions, for three months, to each of Us, which with roots we perhaps may raise, would in some measure make us able, to cutt Wood, and other, Lumber, against, and during the Winter, to provid for us and poor Famelys, till a further Harvest, which would prove a great benefit to the Country in General by Keeping the Fronteers Strongly, Settled and Safe avert charge and Trouble, which would come upon the Provins; by the multitude of so many poor souls, also benefit to the Western; by supplying that part with fire Wood and other Lumber.
        We humbly repose our self's unto
        Your Honours Mercy and shall in Duty bound forever pray.

Maltheus Eichhorn	Mattheis Hoffseess
Heinrich Seitter	Jacob Wolfarth
Burnhart Nikhle	Frank Miller
Jung Mattdeis Eichhorn	Jacob Seergit (Siegrist ??)
Honratt Seitter	Johan Jost Weber
Jacob Heun —— Seegrist	
Jung Bernhart Nikhle	Ludwich Herbst
Johannes Gross	Johannes Morhart (?)
Girtthin Seittlinger	Joachim Bornheimer
Walter Miller	Anthon Burkhard
Christian Wolffsgruber	Johann Hennrich Kohler
Johan Dieter Biergenbaur	Michel Heissler
Johanness Hidenheim	Gorg Hubene
Gottfriet Oberlak	Siemon Miele
Johannes Genther	Johann Martin Ulmer
Johannes Walss	Frantz Eissner
Johannes Walth (?)	Balthasar Kassener (Sassener?)
Johann Georg Reid	Johann Michael Reid
Lorentz Seitz	Philipp Vogler
Christianuss Klein	Paulus Tochtermann
Jakob Umbraths (?)	David Rominger
Jakob Eichhorn	Michael Rominger
Jerg Karmer	Conrad Daniel Walther
Jost Heinrich Miller	JOH . . . . . (illegible)
Jacob Reed (= Ried)	Johannes Kuntzel
Paul Kuhn	Fredrich Kuntzel
Hanss Jacob Jung	Bernharth Kuntzel
Johan Strater	Johan Danial Vilhauer
Kunrath (Konrad) Roth	Jerg Roth
Henrich Georg	Kabssler Glauss
David Holtzapple	

137

TAKEN FROM THE FLY LEAF

OF THE ORIGINAL FAMILY BIBLE

OF JOHAN AND MARIA ELEANORA LOWEN ZOLLNER
(Currently in the Possession of Pauline Levensaler of Concord, New Hampshire)

Christina Löwen Zöllner — Born: August 4, 1755

Maria Löwen Zöllner — Born: November 17, 1761

Katerina Löwen Zöllner — Born: July 8, 1764

Anna Margaretha Löwen Zöllner — Born: September 30, 1766

Elizabeth Löwen Zöllner — Born: July 1, 1769

Georg Löwen Zöllner — Born: April 15, 1773

Adam Löwen Zöllner — Born: April 15, 1773

Johan Löwen Zöllner — Born: January 30, 1775

Peter Löwen Zöllner — Born: April 16, 1778

Not listed on the flyleaf, but on the reverse side of the page:

John Jacob Löwen Zöllner — Born: November 8, 1768

138

ENTRIES FOUND IN THE JOHN LEVENSELLER

FAMILY BIBLE

(Bible now in the possession of The Waldoboro Historical Society)
On the page in the middle of a 1824 Bible, marked **BIRTHS:**

Married:	*January 8, 1799*	
	Born:	*Died:*
Johan Levenseler	January 30, 1775	February 14, 1845
Katharine Levenseler	February 10, 1782	September 16, 1847
Aaron Levenseler	May 30, 1801	July ------ 1872
Moses Levenseler	February 22, 1804	March 29, 1882
Absalom Levenseler	June 27, 1806	October, 1882
Mary Leonora Levenseler	March 8, 1809	November 26, 1858
John Adam Levenseler	March 23, 1812	August, 1874
Cyrus Levenseler	November 8, 1814	July 30, 1890
Hector Brown Levenseler	April 12, 1817	November 15, 1899
Henry Levenseler	March 25, 1820	May 22, 1864
Harriet Alamanda Levenseler	April 4, 1822	
Washington Levenseler	May 14, 1825	February 11, 1843

On the page opposite this list: **Moses Levenseler**

ENTRIES FOUND IN THE PHILLIP BENNER

FAMILY BIBLE
(Bible now in the possession of Ms. Muriel Mitchell of Washington, ME)

Marriages:

Florance C. Levenseler	Sept. 23, 1874
Florance C. Folsom	Oct. 31, 1884
Lena McLoon	Feb. 8, 1913
James McLoon	Nov. 20, 1931
Muriel McLoon	Nov. 6, 1948
Muriel Mitchell	Jan. 19, 1980

Births:

John A. Levensaller	March 12, 1812
Ely M. Levensaller	Jan. 3, 1816
Lena S. Folsom	Aug. 20, 1878
William J. Weeks	May 27, 1855
James W. McLoon	Jan. 26, 1905
Muriel T. McLoon	Oct. 27, 1931
Alonzo Levenseler	Aug. 15, 1840
Miron Levenseler	May 1, 1842
Oris Levenseler	1844
Azro Levenseler	Sept. 10, 1846
Susan Levenseler	July 24, 1850
Florance Levenseler	Sept. 23, 1857
Lizzie Levenseler	June 22, 1870
John A. Levenseler	Nov. 11, 1874
Chester A. Levenseler (Benner)	1882
Mary Ellen Levensaler	Oct. 29, 1869
Walter Lincoln Levenseler	Jan. 15, 1873

Deaths:

Miron Levensaler	April 11, 1843
John A. Levensaler	Aug. 23, 1874
Florance C. Weeks	April 3, 1934
Ely M. Levenseller	Dec. 28, 1906
Susan Benner	Aug. 1941
William Weeks	July 1929
Lena S. Benner	Jan. 3, 1951
James McLoon	Oct. 1966

EXCERPTS FROM WALDOBORO TOWN RECORDS

1765 - 1923

MARRIAGES

DATE	HUSBAND	WIFE
03/31/178	John Benner	Margert Levensaler
12/25/1787	John Newbert	Mary Levenzelner
10/08/1792	George Shuman	Keaty Levensaler
08/15/1793	George Proct	Betty Levensaler
01/22/1793	Godfrey Levensaler	Christiana Snowdeal
05/05/1798	Adam Levensaler	Polly Turner (Tomaston)
02/23/1799	Andrew Hoffses	Betsey Levenseller
01/10/1803	Peter Levenseller	Betsey Kinsel
12/01/1817	Isaac Skinner	Catherine Levensaler
10/07/1820	Adam Shuman	Elizabeth Levenseller
01/1823	Fred Overlock	Mary Levenzeller
11/17/1825	Albert Willet	Agnes Levenseller
10/27/1827	Peter Benner	Mary Ann Levenseller
01/02/1832	Edward Benner	Mary Leonora Levenseller
05/10/1832	Leonard Levensaler	Evelina Benner
03/30/1833	John Levensaler II	Dorothy Mink
10/13/1837	Miathias Moody	Susan Levensaler
01/01/1838	Aaron Levensaler	Mary Benner
06/22/1839	John A. Levensaler	Elcey M. Benner
11/28/1840	Charles S. Soule	Elisabeth Levensaler
02/06/1846	Warren Fowles	Harrieta Levensaler
09/19/1846	Hector Levensaler	Louisa I. Genthner
03/21/1848	Irving Calderwood	Emily I. Levensaler
08/26/1848	Charles Levensaler	Esther M. Crammer
01/22/1855	Ezra Geuthner	Catherine A. Levensaler
01/16/1856	Charles F. Smith	Rhoda A. Levensaler
01/05/1856	Ludlow Levensaler	Lenora E. Achorn
05/16/1857	Sterling Davis	Harriet A. Levensaler
05/09/1858	Isaac Keen Jr.	Susan Levensaler
07/09/1860	Charles H. Auld	Mary J. Levensaler
10/12/1861	David Cakes Jr.	Lucy Levensaler
05/10/1862	William Levensaler	Laura Cunningham

MARRIAGES

DATE	HUSBAND	WIFE
01/02/1864	Barden Turner	Mary H. Levensaler
03/15/1866	Elijah S. Levensaler	Martha E. Lash
05/04/1867	William Levensaler	Lizzie J. Waltz
02/28/1874	Thomas Fitzgerald	Hattie E. Levensaler
10/05/1874	Edward F. Levensaler	Jane B. Willett
04/25/1877	Murray F. Benner	Susan A. Levensaler
05/12/1877	Oris Levensaler	Elodia A. Lash
04/06/1879	William Eugley	Lenora Levensaler
07/11/1880	Levi S. Pitcher	Aldana C. Levensaler
02/11/1881	Moses W. Levensaler	Mary E. W. Miller
07/04/1882	Elmer E. Newbest	Ada B. Levensaler

BIRTHS

DATE	NAME	FATHER
02/11/1765	Peter	Christopher Levensaler
12/08/1766	Mari Catharina	Christopher Levensaler
09/08/1768	Jacob	Christopher Levensaler
05/13/1769	Godfrey	Christopher Levensaler
08/26/1771	Christopher	Christopher Levensaler
05/26/1773	Batty	Christopher Levensaler

DEATHS

(Buried in the Rural Cemetery)

DATE	NAME	AGE/D.O.B.
06/09/1862	Elizabeth Levensaler	81yrs. 1mo. 5 days
02/08/1863	Peter Levensaler	84yrs. 10mo. 2.days
12/19/1869	Hudson Levensaler	21yrs. 4mo.
06/13/1870	Bersha Levensaler	Born March 6, 1813
08/24/1870	Louisa Levensaler	41yrs. 5mo.
02/27/1872	Jermina Levensaler	Born May 13, 1818

DEATHS

(Buried in the Commery Cemetery)

DATE	NAME	AGE/D.O.B.
1835	Sally Levensaler	36 yrs.
April 11, 1843	Miron Levensaler	11 mos.
1844	Amos Levensaler	23 yrs.
1844	George Levensaler	72 yrs.
1845	John Levensaler	Born 1775
1847	Katherine Levensaler	Born 1782
1852	Nancy M. Levensaler	Born 1836
1857	Margaret Levensaler	80 yrs.
1858	Roscoe A. Levensaler	Born 1852
May 22, 1864	Henry Levensaler	44 yrs.
September 3, 1871	Elizabeth Levensaler	46 yrs. 5 mos.
1872	Loring Levensaler	72 yrs.
1874	John A. Levensaler	Born 1814
1877	Betha Levensaler	Born 1856
1877	Maud J. Levensaler	Born 1877
1881	Rhoda C. Levensaler	81 yrs.

EXCERPTS FROM THE WALDOBORO TOWN RECORDS
DEATHS 1890-1923

NAME	DATE	AGE	PARENTS	CAUSE OF DEATH
Moses W	03/29/92	88yrs. 1m.7das.		Old Age
Sally	12/31/98	86yrs.10 m.	John Hahn	Cerebral Hemmorage
Hector B.	11/15/99	82yrs. 7m.		Cerebral Hemmorage
Elizah S.	02/05/01	57yrs. 11d	Jacob Levensaler & Caroline Shuman	Chronic Gastritis.
Harry	02/25/05	65yrs.		Tuberculosis
Julia	08/01/0	44yrs.9m. 26d.	Martin Willey & Elsie Collomore	Peritonitis
Eelcy	12/28/06	90yrs. 11m.	Philip Benner	Hemipligia
Florence B.	03/04/09	15yrs. 3mos.	Edward Levensaler & Mary L. Hahn	Pneumonia
Moses W.	10/01/14	67yrs. 2m. 19d.	Moses Levensaler & Sally Hahn	Carcenoma of Colon
Orris	09/03/15	71yrs. 7m.18d.	John A. Levensaler & Elcy Benner	Angina Pectoris
Mary E.	05/07/17	71yrs. 10m.10d.	Otis Miller & Francis Benner	
William H.	07/04/19	78yrs. 9m. 16d.	Moses Levensaler & Sally Hahn	Gangreen both Legs
Azro	11/11/22	76yrs. 7m.7d.	John A. Levensaler & Elcy Benner	Unknown
Wilford	04/24/23	68yrs.	Ludlow Levensaler & Leonora Achorn	Pneumonia
Eward F.	08/15/23	78yrs. 1m. 9d.	Moses Levensaler & Sally Hahn	General Disability

Excerpt From The Boston Chronicle - Monday, September 9, 1799

Deaths

In this town, on Monday last, very suddenly, Mr. *Adam Leavensealer, AE 69, of Waldoborough*

Excerpt From The Boston Post: Monday, April 18, 1854

Disasters

During a gale on Monday(this) morning, the schooner, Orbit, Capt. Miller from Waldoboro for Boston, with a cargo of lumber, went ashore on Point Alderton bar about 9 O=clock. The Captain and crew were taken off by the life boat and landed at Hull. The vessel lies in a bad position, and will probably go to pieces. Person are on the beach taking charge of such parts of the wreck as they wash ashore.

Excerpt From The Boston Post: Tuesday, April 19,1854

Disasters

Schooner Orbit, Miller, from Waldoboro, for Salem, which went ashore on Point Alderton, will be a total loss. No insurance, The cargo of wood has been landed at Hull.

LEVENSALER EARLY WAR RECORD

FRENCH AND INDIAN WAR

John Leavinfeyler member of Jonas Fitch Company of Home Guards
Entered: May 16, 1757   Discharged: October 31, 1757
Tour of Duty: 24 weeks 6 days   PAY: 8 Pounds 1 Shilling

WAR OF 1812

Peter Levenseller - - - member of 3rd Regiment (Thatchers
Massachusetts Militia)
Entered: September 4, 1814   Discharged: September 10, 1814
Tour of Duty: 7 days   Pay: 1 Dollar 86 Cents
Rank: Private

Served in Captain Philip Kiezor's Company of infantry in Lieutnant
Col.sl Samuel Thatchers' Regiment. Orders were to: Rendezvous at
Waldoborough, September 4, 1814, march to Camden, thence back to
Waldobrough, and there discharged.

CIVIL WAR

Elijah S. Levenseller - - - member of Company "E", Twentieth Maine
Infantry
Entered: August 29, 1862   Discharged: June 4, 1865
Tour of Duty: 33 months   Died: February 5, 1901 in
Waldoboro

Participated in every battle the regiment was in; faught at Antietam
and Appomattux.

Henry Levenseller - - - Member of Company "A", Twenty-second
Massachusetts Infantry
Entered: August 29, 1862   Died: May 22, 1864
Tour of Duty: 21 months

Received a gunshot wound in the arm at the battle of Fair Oaks,
Virginia mortally wounded at Laurel Hill, Virginia. Died in
Frederricksberg, Virginia at the end of the Wilderness Campaign.

Taken from the LINCOLN COUNTY NEWS, 1885, by W.H.L.
(Probably Wm. H. Levensaler)

It was at the battle of Laurel Hill, the 20 Me. was in company with the 118 Penn. on the skirmish line. While waiting after drinking coffee and eating pork and hard tack, Chas. Keizer said to Henry Levensaler of the 32nd Mass. "Let's make more coffee and eat our last supper. This they did after which they were ordered to the front, formed line and advanced. Now as we were making our way towards the enemy through a pine thicket, night was creeping upon us. Soon dusk and then darkness. We supposed a skirmish line was in our advance, but they were not there. Entirely unprotected we were feeling our way in the darkness. Just now we heard an order to drop, and as we did so we could hear a rustle, and they were upon us. There was a fearful conflict, men firing in each others' faces. I don't think they were more than eight or ten feet distant when the first shot was fired. Lieut Keene told me after the battle that the first warning he had was when a rebel officer came upon him and said, "Surrender, you damned Yankee sons of bitches!" At this he disappeared and I think it very doubtful he give orders after that. He was probably riddled by a dozen bullets. Keizer was at my right hand on his knees and when they returned the fire he fell against me. I suppose he was shot dead and then we lost one of our best men. No braver man ever shouldered a musket. At the same time Henry Levensaler was also shot, and after the battle the conversation just before going in occurred to me: "Lets eat our last supper!"

William H. Levenseller - - - member of Company "E", Twentieth Maine Infantry

Entered: August 29, 1862   Discharged: June 4, 1865

Tour of Duty: 33 months   Rank: Corporal

Detached to a division of sharpshooters on August 1, 1864. was on the skirmish line in every battle from Petersberg to Appomattox.

Henry C. Levensaler - - - Member of Nineteenth Maine Regiment

Entered as an assistant surgeon, promoted to surgeon in the Eighth Maine Regiment.

EXCERPTS FROM THE WALDOBORO, MAINE

TOWN CENSUS - 1906

HEAD OF HOUSEHOLD	RESIDENTS	OCCUPATION
Lewis K. Levensaler		
Lenora Day		Housewife
	Velma F. (Daughter)	
	Marion E.(Daughter)	
	Hazel M. (Daughter)	
	Harold D. (Son)	
	Doris R. (Daughter)	
	Alton S. (Son)	
Azro Levensaler		Painter and Paper Hanger
Emma A. (Campbell)		Housewife
	Walter L. (Son)	Carpenter in Everett,MA
	Mary E. m.(Beal)	Post card tinseler
		4 French Terrace
		Roxbury, Mass.
W.F. Levensaler		Truckman
	George L. (Son)	Laborer
G.L. Levensaler		Laborer
Lilla M. (Davis)		Housewife
Moses W. Levensaler		Clothier
Mary E. (Miller)		Housewife
	Ruth E. (Daughter)	
Oris Levensaler		Marble Worker
Sarah D. (Magune)		Housewife
William H. Levensaler		Merchant
Lizzie J. (Waltz)		Housewife
	Fred A. (Son)	Electrician (Portland)
		Guy A. (Son) Clerk
Edwin F. Levensaler		Farmer
Lizzie M. (Hahn)		Housewife
	Florence B.(Daughter)	
	Laura (Daughter)	
	Martha (Lash)	Housewife
Elise Levensaler (Benner)		Housewife
Alonzo m. (Wharfinger)		

Reginald French Papers

From Papers Collected Over the Years by Reginald French of Waldoboro
Transactions between Isaac G. Reed and John Levenseller:

Isaac G. Reed to John Levenseller

1823	Wood	$3.00	2 pigs	$2.25	$5.25
1824	Cash at Warren Court				$4.00
	1 Load of Wood to Mrs Achorn				

$1.50

        Use of Oxen $4.00

                                      $14.75

July 27, 1824   Received Payment: John Levenseller

March 29, 1826

Isaac G. Reed received of John Levenseller
    for coal - potatoes and Rye $5.00

                Received payment: John Levenseller

Isaac G. Reed to John Levenseller
November 1826

	For	2 Bushels Peas	$2.00
	For	Turnips	$2.00

December 1826

	For	44 Baskets Coal	$3.52
	For	1 Barrel Cabbage	$3.00
			$13.33

February 7, 1827   Received Payment: John Levenseller

Reginald French Papers

From Papers Collected Over the Years by Reginald French of Waldoboro

---

Mechanics Association - Waldoboro
Share No. 1 $100 Dollars

Be it known that Jane Ann Reed is entitled to one share in the Mechanics Association. Transferable only at the store of the company. Witness the signature of the agent of the Mechanics Association of Waldoboro this eleventh day of December A.D. 1854

Signed: John A. Levensaler, Agent

Court Summons
October 10, 1840

Lincoln County, October 12, 1840. By virtue of this warrant, I attached a pen to the   property of the within named Berry and gave him a summons in hand for his appearance in court

Singed: J. A. Levensaller   Deputy Sheriff

Fee for Sheriff:
   $.25
   $.04
   $.29

Waldoboro   September 30, 1805

For value received, I promise to pay George Soke on his order, one dollar and fifty cents on demand.

Attested: George Demouth   Signed: George Levensaler

From Papers Collected Over the Years by Reginald French of Waldboro

---

August 17, 1811

Godfrey Levenseller to Abner Keen

For Setting Two Old Shoes	$.25
For Mending Scythe	$.25
For Setting One New Shoe	$.41
	$.91

May 6, 1847

Lincoln Levensalor of Thomaston was paid $11 for fire damage to his house, by Thomaston Mutal Fire Insurance Company.

December 11, 1857

John Levenseler Jr. of Washington, Maine sued by George Demouth of Waldoboro. Owed $54.32. his farm house was attached for payment.

A Deed Executed By John A. Levensaler in 1847

Know all Men by these Presents, That

I, Henry Levensaler of Waldoboro, County of Lincoln in the State of Maine

in consideration of the sum of **Sixty Dollars** *paid by Warren Benner of same*

Waldoboro, County of Lincoln in the State of Maine the receipt whereof I do

hereby acknowledge, do hereby give, grant, bargain, Sell, and Convey unto

the said **Warren Benner** *his heirs and assigns forever. A certain lot or parcel of land situated in said Waldoboro Beginning at the Southern corner of a certain lot of land conveyed to George W Nebort by Henry Levensaler. Thence a northerly course by the land of said Newbort about one hundred rods to the land owned by Charles Flatmer. Thence Easterly course to the land of Moses Levensaler. Thence for Southerly course by said land to the land of Ebner Mink. Thence a Westerly course by said land to the first mentioned bounds, containing thirty acres more or less, reserving the right of cutting and removing the lumber as specified in a lease given to Warren Fowles and Nathan Barr. And also the undivided half of a lot of land situated in Waldoboro and bounded as follows: beginning at a swamp and thence near Warren Benners house on the Southeast side of the county road, thence running a Southeasterly course by the land of Warren Benner to the meadow brook, thence down said brook to the Mink Road, so called, thence up said road to the County road, then on said road to the first mention bounds, containing one half acre more or less.*

TO HAVE AND TO HOLD, *the aforegranted and bargained Premises, with all the privileges and appurtenances thereof, to the said* **Warren Benner** *his heirs and assigns, to their use and behoof forever. And I do covenant with the said* **Warren Benner** *his heirs and assigns, that I am lawfully siezed in fee of the Premises; that they are free of all incumbrances; that I have good right to sell and convey the same to the said* **Warren Benner** *to hold as forsaid; and that I and heirs shall and will* **WARRANT AND DEFEND** *the same to the said* **Benner** *his heirs and assigns forever, against the lawful claims and demands of all persons.*

In Witness Whereof, the said *Henry Levensaler*

and wife of the said

In testimony of her relinquishment of her right of Dower, in the above described premises, have herunto set

hand and seal this *Fifteenth* day of *June* in the year of our Lord

one thousand eight hundred and forty *seven*

SIGNED, SEALED AND DELIVERED
IN PRESENCE OF

John A. Levensaler   *Henry Levensaler*

Lincoln   ss.   *June 15th*   184 **7** Personally appearred

the above named *Henry Levensaler*

and acknowledged the above instrument to be *his* free act and deed. Before me,

John A. Levensaler JUSTICE OF THE PEACE.

INDEX TO LAND RECORDS 1786 - 1856
LINCOLN COUNTY - WISCASETT, MAINE

DATE	BOOK	PAGE	GRANTOR	GRANTEE
1786	19	176	John A. Levenseller	Thomas Plum
1788	22	75	John Benner	John A. Levenseller
1796	37	239	John A. Levenseller	Bernard Freeman
1798	42	103	David Shibles	Adam Levenseller
1798	42	86	David Shibles	Adam Levenseller
1799	44	198	John A. Levenseller	George Levenseller
1799	44	198	John Shuman	George Levenseller
1799	44	210	John A. Levenseller	John Levenseller
1800	45	127	George Levenseller	Peter Light
1801	47	188	Godfrey Levenseller	John Heal
1801	47	233	Godfrey Levenseller	Charles Feyler
1801	48	143	John Dilleway	Adam Levenseller
1804	54	17	Benjamin Cushing	Stephen Levenseller
1806	62	110	Henry Knox	John Levenseller
1807	63	92	Thomas Shibles	Adam Levenseller
1809	72	213	Henry Knox	George Levenseller
1810	119	140	William Sullivan	John Levenseller
1810	75	76	Jerimiha Levenseller	John Foster
1813	53	157	John Levenseller	Henry Knox
1820	109	243	William Sullivan	John Levenseller
1821	113	236	George S. Miller	Godfrey Levenseller
1824	125	193	Joseph Ludwig	Joseph Levenseller

DATE	BOOK	PAGE	GRANTOR	GRANTEE
1824	127	66	John Levenseller	Charles Benner
1824	127	155	Adam Levenseller	Barton Levenseller
1825	130	397	Job Rider	Adam Levenseller
1826	138	27	Daniel Rose	Barton Levenseller
1826	140	333	Joseph Sprague	Lincoln Levenseller
1827	140	334	William Keith	Lincoln Levenseller
1828	145	397	Stimpson Brown	Barton Levenseller
1828	147	15	Lincoln Levenseller	Thomaston Bank
1830	147	321	Barton Levenseller	John Gleason
1830	150	59	Adam Levenseller	Caleb Levenseller
1830	150	202	Godfrey Levenseller	Thomas Appleton
1830	150	438	Peter Mink	Moses Levenseller
1830	150	443	William Sullivan	John Levenseller
1830	150	444	James Woltz	Moses Levenseller
1830	152	94	Lincoln Levenseller	John Dresser
1831	153	212	Barton Levenseller	Caleb Levenseller
1831	153	467	William Sullivan	George Levenseller
1831	154	190	Jacob Hahn	Aaron Levenseller
1832	155	43	Owen Keegan	Lincoln Levenseller
1832	155	66	Owen Keegan	Lincoln Levenseller
1832	155	68	Owen Keegan	Lincoln Levenseller
1832	155	159	Atwood Levenseller	Ben Foster
1832	155	172	Robert Foster	Atwood Levenseller

DATE	BOOK	PAGE	GRANTOR	GRANTEE
1832	155	219	Joe Colson	Caleb Levenseller
1832	155	235	John Dresser	Lincoln Levenseller
1832	156	171	Edward O'Brien	Lincoln Levenseller
1832	156	432	John Levenseller	Moses Levenseller
1833	157	379	James Woltz	Moses Levenseller
1833	158	186	John Levenseller	Peter Schwartz
1833	159	115	John Levenseller	James Creamer
1833	159	118	George Levenseller	John Hahn
1833	159	458	John Levenseller	Moses Levenseller
1833	159	460	Thomas Atkinson	Lincoln Levenseller
1833	159	463	Lincoln Levenseller	Thomas Atkinson
1834	161	001	Caleb Levenseller	Georges Ins. Co.
1834	161	171	Barton Levenseller	Wilson Life Ins.
1834	161	291	George Levenseller	Leonard Levenseller
1834	162	268	Robert Foster	Levenseller S&A
1834	162	280	Levenseller S&A	Robert Foster
1835	163	86	Alex Palmer	Aaron Levenseller
1835	163	173	Jane Kaler	George Levenseller
1835	163	175	Phillip Benner	George Levenseller
1835	163	177	John Levenseller	William Penham
1835	163	568	Rober Foster	Lincoln Levenseller
1835	164	143	Davis, Bates,Turo	Lincoln Levenseller
1837	168	294	Peter&George Light	John K. Levenseller

DATE	BOOK	PAGE	GRANTOR	GRANTEE
1839	172	007	William Sproul	John A. Levenseller
1839	172	008	Leonard Levenseller	William Levenseller
1839	172	232	John Levenseller	Jacob Levenseller
1840	173	499	George Levenseller	Lawrence Levenseller
1840	174	516	John A. Levenseller	John Bulfinch
1841	175	255	Charles Benner	Henry Levenseller
1841	175	257	Charles Benner	Moses Levenseller
1842	177	173	Abraham Cole	John A. Levenseller
1842	177	478	John Levenseller	Elizabeth Shuman
1844	181	372	Moses Levenseller	John Levenseller
1844	181	373	John Levenseller	Henry Levenseller
1844	181	374	John Levenseller	Moses Levenseller
1846	184	452	Nathan Barnard	Moses Levenseller
1846	185	53	Moses Benner	Aaron Levenseller
1846	185	54	William Sproul	Aaron Levenseller
1846	185	55	Aaron Levenseller	H. McCobb
1847	187	43	George Sproul	Aaron Levenseller
1847	187	44	Aaron Levenseller	John Kaler
1848	188	259	Aaron,John,Cyrus	John Willett
1849	190	612	Moses & Henry	Warren Fowls
1849	191	449	John A. Levenseller	Cyrus Levenseller
1850	192	51	Henry Levenseller	Warren Benner
1850	192	249	Hector Levenseller	Jane Benner

DATE	BOOK	PAGE	GRANTOR	GRANTEE
1853	199	13	Hector Levenseller	Andrew Genthner
1853	200	172	Jane A. Levenseller	Charles Willet
1855	206	97	Jane A. Levenseller	Notice of Foreclose
1856	207	328	Jane A. Levenseller	Caroline Levenseller
1856	207	329	Jacob Levenseller	Jane A. Levenseller

BIBLIOGRAPHY FROM THE MAINE HISTORICAL SOCIETY

974.1s Waldoborough, Maine - History
H629.1Waldo, Samuel, 1696-1759.
Translation of Gen. Waldo's circular 1753:
with an introduction by John Locke. (In
Collections of the Maine Historical Society,
Portland, 1859 23cm. (1st ser.) V.6 p.(319-
332) Issued in Germany to attract settler's
to the owner's lands. (nowWaldoborough)

M Waldoborough (Maine) -- History
W147.4 Waldoboro, Me. The centnennial
celebration of the incorporation of
Waldoboro, Maine. July 4, 1873. Pub. by
George Bliss. Bangor, B. A. Burr, printer,
1873. 52 pp. FW29.W1W2

Mc Waldoboro, Maine--Methodist
W147.4ChurchHistory. Keene, Jessie L
History of the Waldoboro Village Methodist
Church, Waldoboro,Maine. 1957.
Mimeograph. 12p.

387 Waldoboro, Maine--Ships
Am35.1 Goddard, Robert H. I., Jr.
V.4 The passing of the five-masters. (In The
American Neptune, v. 4, no. 1, Jan. 1944,
P.45)

Waldoboro Folks. 1917Waldoboro Boston
Club. The first get together banquet of the
Waldoboro-Boston Club.

Mc Waldoborough (Maine)--Churches
147.2 (Moravian) Jordan, John Woolf
Sketch of the Moravian settlement as Broad
Bay Waldoborough, Maine. Bethlehem, Pa.
The Comenius Press, 1891. 12p (pam.)
(Moravian Historical Society Transactions,
v.4, pt. 1)

Waldoborough, ME. --Genealogy.
929.1 Hurst, Charles W.
Am35.2 French and German immigrants
into V.43 Boston, 1751. In The American
No. 3 Genealogist v.43 no.3 (July 1967)
p.168-

Waldoboro, Maine -- History.
M050 Barter, J. Malcolm.
072 Waldoboro. (In Down East,
v.11,V.11no. 9 June, 1965, p. 36-39, 49-
52.)

M Waldoborough, Maine-- History
W147.9 (McVicar, C Warner) ed.
Waldoborough's history, a brief history of a
beautiful downeast town on Maine's mid-
coast. Waldoboro, Maine, Waldoborough
historical society, (1971?) 16 p. illus., map.
23 cm. Cover title: Signed by Warner
McVicar, editor, June, 1971: p 15.
"Selected bibliography": p.16

M Waldoborough, (Maine)-- History
W147.3 Miller, Samuel Lylewellyn;
(Articles on the history of Waldoborough,
Maine. Excerpts from the Lincoln County
News, 187- (?), (scrap book)

M Waldoboro, (Maine)--History
W147.5 Miller, Samuel L. History of the
town of Waldoboro, Maine by Samuel L.
Miller ... (Wiscasset, Emerson, printer,
1910) 281 p. Front (port) plates.23cm

M Waldoboro, Maine--History
W147 Pitcher, Fred Sketch of Waldoboro,
Maine. Written by Fred A. Pitcher. Typed by
Georgianna Lilly, Hallowell, Maine. 11p.
Typescr.

M Waldoboro, Maine--History
W147.2 Pohlman, H.N.,D.D.
The German colony and Lutheran church in
Maine; an address delivered before the
Historical Society of the Lutheran Church,
at its meeting in Washington, D.C., May 14,
1869. Gettysburg, J. E.Wible, 1869. 24 p.
(Pam.)

M Waldoboro, Maine--History
W147.7 Stahl, Jasper J 1886-
History of old Broad Bay and Waldoboro,
Portland, Me., Bond Wheelwright Co. 1956.
2v. Illus.,ports., maps. 25cm Bibliographical
footnotes.

929.1 Waldoborough, Maine--Genealogy
Am35.2 Hurst, Charles W.
V.44 German settlers at Broad Bay, No.2
Maine, 1757 In the The American
Genealogist, v.44, no.2 (April 1968) p. 127-
128

974.1s Waldoborough, (Maine)--History
H629.1 Starman, John William, 1773-
1854 Some account of the German
settlement, in Waldoborough. By Rev. Mr.
Starman. And a biographical sketch of Mr.
Starman. By Hon. Nath'l Groton. (In
collections of the Maine Historical Sociey.
Portland, 1857. 23cm (1st ser.) V. 5, p.
(401-411)

M --------------- (Same. Excerpt from
W147.1 Maine History Society.
Collections,Series, 1. V.5, 1857, p. 400
(pam.)1 Germans in Waldoborough,Mc. 2
Waldoborough, Me.— Hist. 1. Groton,
Nathaniel, 1791-1858

The Germans in Maine Thompson,
Garrett W. (Excerpts from the
Pennsylvannia-German Vol. 12 no.
10,11,12, Oct.,Nov,Dec, 1911)

SOCIAL SECURTIY DEATH RECORDS
FEBRUARY – 2000

NAME	BORN	DIED	ISSUING STATE
Abram Levensailor	06/11/1914	04/1973	Maine
Archie Levensailor	07/09/1894	05/1968	Maine
Arthur Levensailor	05/29/1924	09/1986	Maine
Bertha Levensailor	06/04/1918	02/24/1999	Maine
Blanche Levensailor	05/20/1905	11/14/1993	New York
Boss Levensailor	02/22/1919	03/11/1999	Texas
Cleo Levensailor	08/27/1920	08/23/1995	Maine
Clifton Levensailor	06/05/1904	05/18/1989	Massachusetts
Edric Levensailor	10/14/1939	02/1982	Maine
Emily Levensailor	12/16/1878	04/1974	Maine
Eunice Levensailor	07/31/1922	01/03/1990	Texas
Everett Levensailor	05/03/1908	06/1977	New York
Forrest Levensailor	12/04/1909	11/13/1993	California
Harry Levensailor	07/06/1914	12/1966	Texas
Irving Levensailor	06/22/1912	07/03/1998	Maine
James Levensailor	06/24/1970	06/21/1997	New York
Jean Levensailor	08/12/1921	03/15/1990	Wisconsin
Joe Levensailor	10/17/1916	02/1979	Texas
John Levensailor	04/04/1914	05/11/1997	Maine
Julias Levensailor	12/09/1912	02/1984	Texas
Leonard Levensailor	09/24/1900	06/1972	New York
Lillie Levensailor	07/18/1912	09/1986	Texas
Mabel Levensailor	12/18/1904	01/1987	Maine
Mabel Levensailor	01/16/1891	02/1975	Maine
Marjorie Levensailor	04/02/1901	11/1983	Maine
Mary Levensailor	05/20/1906	09/1986	New Jersey
Melvin Levensailor	03/17/1918	04/1964	Maine
Melvin Levensailor	02/12/1928	08/27/1991	Maine
Robert Levensailor	10/25/1925	08/1980	Massachusetts
Velma Levensailor	02/26/1918	01/1982	Maine
Virginia Levensailor	07/30/1934	01/1977	Maine
Virginia Levensailor	12/12/1937	12/1981	Maine
W. Levensailor	02/15/1911	03/1973	Texas
Joseph Levansaler	04/18/1876	06/15/1966	California
Ollie Levansaler	08/21/1888	11/15/1972	California
Russell Levansaler	04/23/1899	11/1969	California

SOCIAL SECURTIY DEATH RECORDS
FEBRUARY-2000

NAME	BORN	DIED	ISSUING STATE
Annie Levensaller	04/08/1894	06/1979	Maine
Clifton Levensaller	10/29/1897	12/1963	Maine
Doris Levensaller	05/09/1915	08/19/1997	Maine
Harold Levensaller	11/19/1900	11/1978	Maine
Katherine Levensaller	09/06/1903	11/1969	Maine
M. Levensaller	12/16/1901	09/19/1989	Maine
Albert Levenseler	08/20/1919	01/1985	Maine
Betty Levenseler	10/07/1929	01/28/1995	Massachusetts.
Irene Levenseler	01/08/1888	05/1977	Maine
Whitman Levenseler	12/29/1913	12/13/1994	N. Hampshire
Arthur Levenseller	07/04/1893	04/1974	Maine
Bonita Levenseller	03/08/1911	12/1979	Washington
Byron Levenseller	07/04/1912	10/1972	Washington
Chester Levenseller	09/02/1913	09/1983	Rhode Island
Christine Levenseller	04/18/1917	06/07/1999	Maine
David Levenseller	10/31/1955	10/13/1996	Maine
Donald Levenseller	07/22/1905	03/1961	Washington
Dorothy Levenseller	02/11/1906	10/06/1998	Maine
Florence Levenseller	08/07/1894	02/1982	Maine
Genevieve Levenseller	02/23/1902	10/1974	Michigan
Paul Levenseller	04/24/1916	02/03/1992	California
Perley Levenseller	02/05/1914	10/1967	Maine
Alton Levensaler	08/11/1904	11/1965	Maine
Arnold Levensaler	12/06/1906	11/1972	Maine
Arthur Levensaler	06/20/1898	06/23/1989	New York
Atwood Levensaler	04/10/1911	02/06/1994	N. Hampshire
Bryant Levensaler	05/31/1911	03/05/1992	Maine
Camilla Levensaler	04/15/1907	02/1970	Maine
Carl Levensaler	05/17/1912	03/07/1994	New York
David Levensaler	01/19/1938	01/29/1992	Maine
Diana Levensaler	08/24/1939	04/15/1990	Maine
Dorothy Levensaler	08/11/1912	04/15/1999	California
Dorothy Levensaler	07/23/1914	03/15/1999	Connecticut
Edith Levensaler	08/05/1904	03/1970	Maine

SOCIAL SECURTIY DEATH RECORDS
FEBRUARY-2000

NAME	BORN	DIED	ISSUING STATE
Gwendolyn Levensaler	03/06/1912	07/15/1997	California
Harold Levensaler	03/15/1902	09/1964	Connecticut
Helen Levensaler	09/29/1902	01/12/1994	New York
Ida Levensaler	03/21/1907	04/20/1997	New York
Iva Levensaler	07/19/1894	06/1987	Maine
James Levensaler	03/27/1876	09/1970	California
James Levensaler	01/07/1918	06/1983	California
James Levensaler	08/13/1907	01/26/1994	California
Joseph Levensaler	10/12/1877	01/1967	California
Judson Levensaler	01/21/1908	12/02/1996	California
Leon Levensaler	07/13/1905	09/04/1995	Mass.
Lewis Levensaler	10/21/1879	10/1974	California
Nina Levensaler	02/17/1903	10/1980	New York
Randall Levensaler	03/01/1906	08/04/1998	New York
Raymond Levensaler	10/10/1899	11/28/1988	New York
Sadie Levensaler	01/19/1894	10/1980	New York
Sophie Levensaler	05/15/1905	11/05/1998	Connecticut
William Levensaler	07/08/1869	07/1968	California
William Levensaler	02/06/1890	02/1983	Maine

MAINE STATE ARCHIVES
MARRIAGE HISTORY 1890-1995

BRIDE	TOWN	GROOM	TOWN	DATE
Vista Levensaller	Dover/Foxcroft	Clifton Smith	Lubec	02/14/23
Annie Hovey	Augusta	Clifton Levensaller	Augusta	12/15/26
Doris London	Randolph	Clifton Levensaller	Augusta	06/13/54
Grace Mank	Waldoboro	Clifton Levensaller	Waldoboro	08/21/20
Lilla Davis	Waldoboro	George Levensaller	Waldoboro	02/24/06
Catherine Mullin	Weymouth CN	Raymond Levensaller	Augusta	10/26/27
Addie Levenseller	Lincolnville	Howard Elms	Belmont	11/02/1893
Annie Levenseller	Bangor	William Thompson	Bucksport	02/24/00
Bessie Levenseller	Dexter	Everett Bagley	Dexter	01/12/03
Effie Levenseller	Bangor	Charles Mason	Corinna	08/10/38
Effie Levenseller	Charleston	Hall Bugby	Charleston	12/24/04
Eula Levenseller	Corinna	Wallace Towle	Corinna	09/29/24
Evelyn Levenseller	Atkinson	Orman Gerry	Dover/Fox.	11/25/25
Flora Levenseller	Holden	Sanford Porter	Old Town	06/06/1895
Georgia Levenseller	Holden	C. Clark	Holden	05/10/1893
Grace Levenseller	Holden	Lester Royal	Dexter	11/23/1898
Ivy Levenseller	Bangor	Harry Mcdonald	Bangor	09/08/20
Jennie Levenseller	Lincolnville	John Morse	Belmont	12/14/1895
Josie Levenseller	Monson	Charles Spaulding	Parkman	09/27/1896
Kelly Levenseller	Waterville	Anthony Couture	Waterville	02/15/85
Kelly Levenseller	Waterville	Pero Mathisen	Waterville	05/31/80
Marg. Levenseller	Searmont	Harold Allenwood	Camden	04/10/38
Mary Levenseller	Rockport	Arthur Beal	Boston MA	11/29/1897
Maud Levenseller	Brewer	Geo. Goodwin	Brewer	01/06/15
M. Levenseller	Levant	Roger Young	Levant	02/14/93
M. Levenseller	Dexter	Stephen White	Dresden	12/14/91
Mildred Levenseller	Holden	Bert Blackman	Rumford	04/21/189
Ruby Levenseller	Dexter	Louis Safford	Dexter	02/21/23
Florence Esler	Sangerville	Arthur Levenseller	Dexter	08/26/22
Ethel Monahan	Waterville	Arthur Levenseller	Dexter	09/11/14
Florence Padham	Sangerville	Arthur Levenseller	Dexter	08/26/22
Cynthia Frautten	Dexter	David Levenseller	Dexter0	3/23/79
Hattie Ludden	Madison	Earl Levenseller	Madison	06/18/54
Hattie Malcolm	Madison	Earl Levenseller	Madison	06/18/54
Marjory Thomas	Atkinson	Ernest Levenseller	Atkinson	10/14/17
Winifred Brown	Bangor	Gorham Levenseller	Bangor	03/01/41
Irene Peaslee	Jefferson	Harold Levenseller	Jefferson	08/05/22
Elfreda Gorham	Bangor	Harry Levenseller	Holden	09/05/06
Gloria Coolidge	Dexter	Jack Levenseller	Dexter	12/05/81
Julia Berry	Searsmont	John Levenseller	Searsmont	01/27/06
Stella Alexander	Hudson	Leslie Levenseller	Hudson	02/06/06
Annie Cook	Bangor	Lester Levenseller	Bangor	08/07/1895
Debra Parent	Waterville	Michael Levenseller	Waterville	04/13/84

MAINE STATE ARCHIVES
MARRIAGE HISTORY 1890-1995

BRIDE	TOWN	GROOM	TOWN	DATE
Leola Jones	Washington	Pearl Levenseller	Washington	02/01/1897
Grace McMahon	Eddington	Percy Levenseller	Holden	12/25/1894
Lura Merrifield	Camden	Walter Levenseller	Rockport	01/01/1895
Blanch Weymouth	Dexter	Willis Levenseller	Dexter	06/30/1897
Andrea Levensaler	Waldoboro	Dwayne Severson	Friendship	09/28/85
Carlene Levensaler	Waldoboro	Frank Taylor	Thomaston	12/31/52
Clara Levensaler	Rockland	Charles Adams	Rockland	11/08/02
Cynthia Levensaler		Richard Laine		08/01/58
Doris Levensaler	Waldoboro	Robert Taupier	S.Hampton	09/10/55
Eliza Levensaler	Thomaston	Edward Carleton	Thomaston	06/20/04
Elouise Levensaler	Washington	Angus McDonald	Wash.	09/19/1893
Elsie Levensaler	Waldoboro	Ruel Eugley	Waldoboro	01/01/35
Eva Levensaler	Thomaston	Maurice Athearn	Thomaston	11/16/12
Geraldine Levensaler	Waldoboro	Lemuel Miller	Cushing	02/01/49
Leola Levensaler	Washington	Fanklin McDonald	Washington	08/27/11
Margaret Levensaler	Eliot	Ralph Titus	Eliot	08/22/24
Margaret Levensaler	Searsmont	Linwood Hilt	Union	07/11/25
Marion Levensaler	Gardiner	Cecil Keene	Gardiner	02/12/27
Mary Levensaler		Benjamin Myers	Boston MA	10/31/06
Rhonda Levensaler	N. Yarmouth	Michael Murphy	Portland	06/20/85
Rhonda Levensaler	N. Yarmouth	Robert Darling	Cumberland	10/25/84
Ruth Levensaler	Waldoboro	Wendell Howard		02/15/14
Ruth Levensaler	Waldoboro	Edwin Redding	Charlotte NC	10/30/08
Terri Levensaler	Conn.	Clayton Nivison	Conn.	09/03/77
Terri Levensaler	Waterville	Conrad Hichborn	Waterville	07/30/88
Violet Levensaler	Waldoboro	Harold Sprague	Waldoboro	06/10/44
Rose Maburg	Rockland	Albert Levensaler	Rockland	06/01/41
Camille Lemanq	Garginer	Alton Levensaler	Waldoboro	02/07/29
Violet Pette	Waldoboro	Arnold Levensaler	Waldoboro	09/16/29
Emma Campbell	Waldoboro	Azro Levensaler	Waldoboro	05/05/01
Marilyn Leonard		Cedric Levensaler		04/26/58
Marilyn Maxcy		Cedric Levensaler		04/26/58
Sharon McNaughton	Waldoboro	David Levensaler	Waldoboro	01/27/55
Mary Hahn	Waldoboro	Edward Levensaler	Waldoboro	01/09/1893
Harriet Wardwell	Rockland	Edwin Levensaler	Rockland	03/23/08
Maud Sharp	Portland	Fred Levensaler	Portland	06/06/00
Sadie Mank	Waldoboro	Guy Levensaler	Waldoboro	11/27/19
Mary Drummond		Harold Levensaler		01/01/62
Sarah Magune	Rockport	Orris Levensaler	Waldoboro	05/11/1892
Diana Soule		Richard Levensaler		07/01/58
Debra Donnell	Waldoboro	Richard Levensaler	Waldoboro	09/26/81
Amella Hart	Washington	Thomas Levensaler	Washington	06/23/03
Amella Maddocks	Washington	Thomas Levensaler	Washington	06/23/03

MAINE STATE ARCHIVES
MARRIAGE HISTORY 1890-1995

BRIDE	TOWN	GROOM	TOWN	DATE
Hilda Levenseler	Rockland	Samuel O'Brien	Rockland	09/27/43
Sheila Levenseler	MA	William Taylor	MA	06/29/91
Edith Howard	Union	Albert Levenseler	Rockland	10/31/48
Lucy Dyer	Rockland	Jon Levenseler	Rockland	02/08/85
Anette Levensailor	Guilford	Robert Moulton	Guilford	10/10/86
Arlene Levensailor	S. Windham	Harvy Durant	Saco	11/29/52
Daisy Levensailor	Houlton	Merval Porter	Houlton	06/29/49
Edie Levensailor		Maurice Hall		12/01/63
Edie Levensailor		Clinton Higgins		09/01/58
Emily Levensailor	Benton	Milland Gilmore	Vassalboro	04/26/19
Frances Levensailor	Houlton	Theodore Tompkins	Houlton	09/08/40
Frances Levensailor	Houlton	Ernest Hopkins	Houlton	01/28/48
Geneva Levensailor	Barnard	Daniel Carroll	Barnard	11/16/31
Genieve Levensailor	Barnard	George Esler	Barnard	03/21/19
Gloria Levensailor		Arlo Hall		04/01/62
Ida Levensailor	Glenburn	Clayton Brawn	Glenburn	04/02/38
Irene Levensailor	Skowhegan	Rodney Cumber	Winthrop	07/21/89
Isabel Levensailor	Sangerville	Lewis Flanders	Sangerville	01/31/32
Jean Levensailor	Houlton	Gordon Barton	Houlton	10/07/78
Jennie Levensailor		Walter Jones		10/17/56
Katherine Levensailor	Sanford	Roger Cote	Sanford	12/24/84
Katherine Levensailor	Sanford	John Corr	Sanford	08/1890
Kathy Levensailor	Houlton	Stephen Clark	Houlton	12/23/78
Linda Levensailor	ME	David Daigler	NY	02/26/83
Mabel Levensailor	Foxcroft	Everett Pond	Foxcroft	08/24/02
Margaret Levensailor		Richard Scott		12/01/62
Margie Levensailor	Clinton	Victor Collins	Benton	02/15/80
Marjorie Levensailor	Anson	Allen Jones	Anson	05/06/95
Mary Levensailor	Atkinson	Allen Meader	Atkinson	10/11/04
Mona Levensailor		Norman Beckwith		06/07/58
Shelley Levensailor	Augusta	Henry Garside	Augusta	05/02/92
Bertha Brown	N. Anson	Abram Levensailor	N. Anson	01/24/53
Bertha Willey	N. Anson	Abram Levensailor	N. Anson	01/24/53
Edie Clement	Sebec	Arthur Levensailor	Atkinson	06/07/30
Merrilee Mitchell	Orono	Brian Levensailor	Orono	02/25/92
Naomie Hanscom	Clinton	Clifton Levensailor	Clinton	04/08/33
Eleanor Lavigne		Edric Levensailor		02/02/62
Joan Stackpole	Parkman	Edric Levensailor	Guilford	10/07/78
Mary Patterson	Lewiston	Ernest Levensailor	Auburn	09/03/1893
Virginia Davies	Houlton	George Levensailor	Houlton	04/18/54
Linda Demerchant	CA	George Levensailor	Houlton	12/10/77
Velma Scott	Vassalboro	Irving Levensailor	Vasselboro	01/29/54
Virginia Robinson		John Levensailor		11/01/59
Betty McAdoo	Clinton	John Levensailor	Clinton	09/28/82

MAINE STATE ARCHIVES
MARRIAGE HISTORY 1890-1995

BRIDE	TOWN	GROOM	TOWN	DATE
Mary Soule	Atkinson	John Levensailor	Atkinson	12/24/06
Amy Brown	Dexter	Lesley Levensailor	Dexter	12/11/04
Cleo Smith	Atkinson	Melvin Levensailor	Atkinson	12/31/38
Nellie Perham	Atkinson	Meritt Levensailor	Atkinson	04/29/1893
Tracie McCormick	NY	Michael Levensailor	NY	06/22/85
Debora Davis	Houlton	Michael Levensailor	Houlton	08/14/82
Christine Adkins	Guilford	Perley Levensailor	Guilford	10/31/36
Christine Chase	Guilford	Perley Levensailor	Guilford	10/31/36
Nellie Barker	Corinth	Perlie Levensailor	Corinth	06/15/03
Jennifer Hardin	OH	Scott Levensailor	Guilford	10/08/88
Sonja Partinen		Stanley Levensailor		06/01/62
Emily Brown	Foxcroft	Stephen Levensailor	Atkinson	02/01/02
Alice Davis	Searsport	Stephen Levensailor	Dexter	07/20/13
Marjorie Morse	Clinton	Stephen Levensailor	Clinton	11/02/43
Marjorie Scoville	Clinton	Stephen Levensailor	Clinton	11/02/43
Emily Smith	Foxcroft	Stephen Levensailor	Atkinson	02/21/02
Lee Tina Roy	Clinton	Stephen Levensailor	Clinton	07/11/92
Mary Partridge	Dover	Thomas Levensailor	Dover	01/16/1898
Mary Williams		Alfred Levansaler		08/18/09
Anne Lash	Thomaston	James Levansaler	Thomaston	11/19/00
Olive Delano	Thomaston	Joseph Levansaler	San Francisco	08/26/01

APPENDIX V

NATIONAL LIST OF LEVENSALER HOUSEHOLDS AS OF AUGUST 19, 1997

THIS LIST WAS USED IN THE SURVEY OF THE SAME YEAR AND IS
TAKEN FROM DATA LISTED ON THE INTERNET PERSON LOCATOR.

NAME	CITY	STATE
M. C. Levensaler	Anchorage	AK
Tom Levensailor	Daphne	AL
A. E. Levensailor	Mobile	AL
Dianna Levenseller	Phoenix	AZ
Don Levensaler	Chico	CA
N. N. Levensaler	Kentfield	CA
John Levensailor	Perris	CA
Randall Levensaler	Oakland	CA
Sandra G. Levensaler	Piedmont	CA
Michael J. Levensaler	San Diego	CA
J. L. & Dorothy Levensaler	San Rafael	CA
B. D. Leveseller	San Francisco	CA
Judson D. Levensaler	Walnut Creek	CA
N. N. Levensaler	Yorkville	CA
S. Levensaler	East Windsor	CT
Gary Levensaler	Haddam	CT
Dwight A. Levensaler	Southington	CT
E. Levenseller	Pace	FL
Walter Levensaler	Acton	MA
Sheila Levenseler	Lexington	MA
P. A. Levensailor	Watertown	MA
John Levensaler	Woburn	MA
Doris Levensaller	Augusta	ME
Aaron Levensailor	Bangor	ME
Michael & Debra Levenseller	Belgrade	ME
Joan Levensailor	Cambridge	ME
L L & John Levensaler	Casco	ME
David & Cynthia Levenseller	Corinna	ME
Christine Levenseller	Dexter	ME
Perley Levenseller	Dexter	ME

NAME	CITY	STATE
C. Levensailor	Ellsworth	ME
Stephen & Tina Levensailor	Fairfield	ME
Stanley A. Levensailor	Glenburn	ME
M. M. Levensailor	Guilford	ME
George Levensailor	Houlton	ME
S. Levensaler	Jefferson	ME
Paul Levensaller	Jefferson	ME
G. J. Levenseller	Lewiston	ME
Mike & Debbie Levensailor	Lisbon	ME
Gary Levensaler	Monson	ME
Dickie Levensaler	Nobleboro	ME
Abram B. Levensailor	North Anson	ME
Susan Levenseler	S. Portland	ME
Dana Levensaler	Waldoboro	ME
Dorothy Levensaler	Waldoboro	ME
Richard D. Levensaler	Waldoboro	ME
D. E. Levenseller	Westbrook	ME
Rob & Deb Levensailor	Bailey	MS
J. Levensailor	Farmington	MO
Byron Levenseller	Grand Forks	ND
Pauline Levensaler	Concord	NH
Whitman & Pauline Levensaler	Concord	NH
C. Levensaler	Epsom	NH
Whitman Levensaler	Meredith	NH
Frank C. Levenseller	Cape May	NJ
K. & D. Levenseller	Vincentown	NJ
Leonard L. Levensailor	Boonville	NY
Charles Levensailor	Boonville	NY
Penny Levensailor	Boonville	NY
Joanne Levensailor	Boonville	NY
W. C. Levensailor	Boonville	NY

NAME	CITY	STATE
Thomas J. Levensailor	Glenfield	NY
Helen Levensailor	Port Leyden	NY
Arnold J. Levensailor	Port Leydon	NY
Traci Levensailor	Syracuse	NY
Ida V. Levensaler	Warrensburg	NY
Hattie Levenseller	Watertown	NY
Brandon & Cari Levenseller	Hillsboro	OR
Leonard Levensailor	Carthage	TN
Jacque Levensailor	Kerriville	TX
Wade Levensailor	Liano	TX
S. L. Levensailor	Liano	TX
Lester Levensailor	Liano	TX
S. Levensailor	Liano	TX
B. S. Levensailor	Liano	TX
Lois Levensailor	Liano	TX
Randy S. Levensailor	Seguin	TX
Ellen L. Levenseller	Alexandria	VA
Jeffery Levensaler	Arlington	VA
Harold & Yvonne Levensailor	Dunnsville	VA
Greg & Gail Levenseller	Brinnon	WA
Clifford Levenseller	Port Orchard	WA
Mike & Allison Levenseller	Pullman	WA
Philp Levenseller	Silverdale	WA
Gerald R. Levenseller	Tacoma	WA

BIBLIOGRAPHY

Annals of the Town of Warren,
Cyrus Eaton, A. M. Masters &
Livermore, Hallowell, 1877.

A Town That Went to Sea,
Aubigne Lermond Packard,
Courier-Gazette, Inc., 1987, From
the Thomaston Historical Society.

Broad Bay Pioneers, Wilford
Whitaker & Gary T. Horlacher,
Picton Press, Camden, Maine,
1998.

Early Eighteenth Century Palatine
Emigration, Walter Allen Knittle
Ph.D., Genealogical Publishing
Co., Inc., Baltimore, 1982.

Emigrants from Baden and
Wurttemberg in the Eighteenth
Century (In Two Volumes),
Brigitte Burkett, Picton Press,
Camden, Maine, 1996.

The Germans In Colonial Times,
Lucy F. Bittinger, Heritage Books,
Inc., 1986.

History of Hope, Maine, Anna
Simpson Hardy, Penobscot Press,
Camden, Maine, 1990.

History of Broad Bay and
Waldoboro (In Two Volumes),
Jasper Jacob Stahl, The Bond
Wheelwright Co., Portland, Maine,
1956.

History of the State of Maine (In
Two Volumes), William D.
Williamson, Hollowell, Glazier,
Masters & Co., 1832.

History of Thomaston, Rockland
and South Thomaston, Maine (In
Two Volumes), Cyrus Eaton,
Hallowell, Masters, Smith & Co.,
1865.

History of the Town of Waldoboro,
Maine, Samuel L. Miller,
Emerson, Wiscasset, 1910.

Personal Letter Dated July 5,
1984, Atwood Levensaler,
Concord, New Hampshire.

Personel Letter Dated Aug. 3,
1989, Martha B. Tompkins,
Waldoboro, Maine.

Personal Letter Dated August 23,
1989, Muriel Mitchell,
Washington, Maine.

Personal Letter Dated September
10, 1997, Pauline Levensaler,
Concord, New Hampshire.

Personel Letter Dated October 20,
1989, Reginald French,
Waldoboro, Maine.

Personal Letter Dated June 17,
1993, W.W. Whitaker, Murray,
Utah.

Sketches of the History of the
Town of Camden, Maine, John L.
Locke, Heritage Books, Inc., 1998.

Warren Cemeteries 1735-1985,
Leland Overlock, Warren
Historical Society, 1985.